Praise for Pejman Ghadimi's
Third Circle Theory

"Third Circle Theory is the real deal and a must read for any entrepreneur!" – **Nellie Akalp, CEO of CorpNet**

"Third Circle Theory is not just a book about business and life, it is an analysis that will reshape the way you think about the path that your life is taking, why is it taking it, and what you can do to affect it. I wish I read this book 20 years ago!" – **Fabio Viviani, Celebrity Chef and Restauranteur**

"If you're not reading this book, and truly taking in what it has to offer, you're missing out and that's sad." – **Tim Sykes, Penny Stock Millionaire**

"One of the best books I have ever read." – **Andy Frisella, CEO of 1st Phorm**

"I recommend this book as a blueprint, outline, or roadmap to a successful life." – **Allen Wong, CEO of Rego Apps**

"Whether you are an entrepreneur or aspire to be one, this is an amazing book." – **Nathan Chan, CEO of Foundr Magazine**

"If you're hitting walls in your business or personal growth, give this book a read and put it into action." – **Jordan Harbinger, CEO of Art of Charm**

"It's a personalized roadmap of your potential in life, created to take you from dreaming to doing, and it took me from a high school student to $40k a month in sales." – **Kiran Ravindra, CEO of Carbon Trim Solutions**

"The Third Circle Theory is on another level. This is a great book for anyone looking to gain knowledge and insight on the many self-proclaimed definitions of success and why some of us achieve a higher level than others." – **Tywane Russell, Professional Body Builder**

"This is true entrepreneurship without the glamour and BS. You can tell it's written by someone who has been there and succeeded." – **Jordan Swerdloff, CEO of ADV1 Wheels**

"Three words that best describes what you will achieve from reading this book: enlightenment, inspiration, and fulfillment. What are you waiting for? Go achieve what others haven't. This book is your shortcut." – **Ted Wynn, CEO of EVS Motors**

"Whether you're new to the game, on the road to success, or already well established, this book is a must." – **Ian Mason, CEO of BuildPath.co**

"A must read for anyone who wants to become anything more than someone's employee." – **Camerous Fous, Penny Stock Millionaire**

THIRD

CIRCLE

THEORY

PURPOSE THROUGH OBSERVATION

SECRET ENTÖÜRAGE

Third Circle Theory
Purpose Through Observation
Secret Entourage
www.SecretEntourage.com

Table of Contents

THE POWER OF DISCOVERY 9

WHY DO YOU EXIST? 13

FAITH VERSUS OPPORTUNITY 15
HOW THE THIRD CIRCLE THEORY WILL HELP YOU 20
WHY THE THIRD CIRCLE THEORY WAS CREATED 21

Third Circle Theory Introduction 25

THE FIRST CIRCLE: THE BIRTH, THE SETTLER, & THE
DREAMER 27

THE SECOND CIRCLE: THE AWAKENING, THE LEADER, &
THE ACHIEVER 33

THE THIRD CIRCLE: THE VISION, THE PURPOSE, & THE
REBIRTH 37

PROGRESSION OF THE MIND 42

THE FIRST CIRCLE 45

ENVIRONMENT 46
BELIEF 51
CHOICE 56
FEAR 59
CONFIDENCE 64
GOALS 67
ENTOURAGE 71
TIME 75

THE SECOND CIRCLE 83

EDUCATION 85
MONEY 91
HABITS 97
EMOTION 105
LEADERSHIP 112
PERCEPTION 118

Table of Contents

THE THIRD CIRCLE 123

    LIFESTYLE.. 125
    VISION 130
    ENTREPRENEUR 133
    LEGACY 136

A SELFLESS FINAL ACT.. 139

    HOW IT APPLIES IN THE REAL WORLD 147
    WHY THE SELF-HELP INDUSTRY WON'T WORK 149
    HOW FULFILLMENT AND PURPOSE ARE DIFFERENT..... 153
    UNDERSTANDING YOUR VALUE 155
    EXPLAINING LIFE'S SPIDER WEB 157
    THE ENTRAPMENT OF SOCIETY.. 160
    THE ROLE OF EDUCATION... 161
    THE ROLE OF GOVERNMENT 162
    THE ROLE OF CORPORATE AMERICA 166
    BREAK YOUR COMFORT ZONE BY CREATING CHANGE 167
    LIVING FOR THE EXPERIENCE OF LIFE ITSELF 172

THE BIRTH OF PURPOSE... 175

THE BIRTH OF AN IDEA 179

FINAL WORDS... 185

ABOUT THE AUTHOR 189

For my mom Shahla,

A woman who never put herself first.

Thank you for showing me a different world.

Preface

When I first came up with the concept of Third Circle Theory, I knew deep inside my heart that this book would become a beacon of hope for many and a voice of reason for others. Throughout my 18 years in business, I always knew that I had a gift for helping people uncover their potential and follow through on their dreams. I was able to guide hundreds of people before the book was released, and I knew that by conceptualizing this theory I would be able to help millions. In the past three years, Third Circle Theory has reached well over 200,000 people and is continuing to grow, helping me fulfill my very own goal and life purpose. As you read and understand the concepts shared in this book, please do not forget that no matter who you are, where you live, what challenges you face, or how tough things get, the answers are and always have been within you. By understanding the Third Circle Theory, I hope that you realize how all of us as human beings are connected, and how limitless we can be when given a sense of purpose.

THIRD CIRCLE THEORY

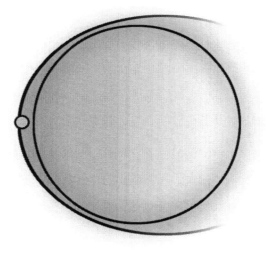

Prologue

What is it that makes certain individuals so much more capable than others? What is it that allows innovation and advancement in the world to take place? Who are those people who hold that capacity, and why can they create the change we all know is needed? Why are these individuals always full of energy, and yet others just always feel lazy?

In my 30 years of life, I have witnessed some pretty amazing things. I have seen people who have lost everything be inspired by a picture drawn on a napkin, and as a result climb back to the very top against all odds. I have witnessed immigrants who barely spoke English rise to executive positions within the system and earn six-figure incomes in less than four years, because someone took a chance on them. But nothing I have seen is more amazing to me than the power of the human mind and its evolution when given a sense of purpose.

I am no psychologist and certainly not a scientist. I know nothing of biology, and quite frankly, did very poorly during my high school years. After just two years in college, I dropped out due to complete boredom — despite being only one course away from finishing my Associate's degree. Many will tell you that foregoing college is a huge mistake, but throughout this book you will understand why education held no relevance in my life.

I could start telling you all about my lifestyle or the possessions I accumulated, which should make you buy into the book itself. But if I did, that by itself would go against the essence of this book's important message. What I will tell you; however, is that the lifestyle I live today is the exact one I want to be living, not the one my initial circumstance had intended for me. The possessions I have today are not a good representation of how I wish to be remembered and hold very little relevance to who I have become.

What did maintain relevance in my life was a group of people who all played a significant role as they entered and exited my life at different stages. These people held no connection to one another except that they were all connected through me; individuals who helped open and broaden my views and vision to the reality of what the world is. They helped shape my life into what it is today.

When things in front of you change and you start seeing more than others, you will question why you are given that ability and what it can all mean. It sparks your philosophical perspective and drives you to think of a powerful word, "**Purpose,**" and to consider what yours is.

For me, the concept of purpose came earlier than most. As an analytical and philosophical person, I was naturally motivated to attempt to understand how and why I was privileged enough to have found my purpose. This self-exploration enabled me to eventually conceive and develop the "**Third Circle Theory,**" a principle of how one person can prepare themselves to find their own purpose.

Finding your purpose is extremely important for yourself and all of those around you. Purposeful individuals are motivated, often more active in society, and most importantly, an inspiration to those around them. The core of what advances this world are those extraordinary people who see it for what it can be, rather than what it is presently. When these essential, purposeful individuals identify where they fit in society, they can help shape the world to mimic their vision of it. Purpose is ultimately the catalytic energy we need to see our vision and ideas come to life. It's the fuel of life and holds the key to fulfillment well above that of money. Even though your purpose cannot ever be proven to have been right or wrong, the powerful energy that emits from someone with the belief that they have found it is the extraordinary feeling that the Third Circle Theory helps you reach.

As you read this book, keep in mind that my goal is to challenge your perspective, not your judgment. There is no right or wrong here, but instead two different ways to look at the exact same thing. Regardless of your ability to adapt immediately to this new way of discovering yourself, just the idea that you are now aware of this alternative viewpoint will open your mind to a new frontier; because perspective is ultimately derived from your knowledge and beliefs (values).

The Power of Discovery

The self-help industry has changed significantly over the past few decades. So much of its focus is based on educating you on how to make money, and in turn those "gurus" make large profits. The Third Circle Theory was created instead to elevate your understanding of purpose and help you find yourself through helping others. It is ultimately the best guide to help you not only define your existence, but also understand the true value of the people around you when factored into the equation of a successful life.

When you think of success today, you might neglect to consider the success of those around you. Instead you think about how your success looks right now, and what it could look like once you have accomplished everything necessary. After you have explored this new way to look at life through this book, you will be able to understand how impactful your observations of life are in the context of your growth. You will also realize how to pull away from the money-chasing rat race. Instead, you will see a new element to success that defines the difference between those who become innovators, creators, and icons versus those who just keep making more money without a purpose.

Have you ever wondered why some businesses like Apple have become so immense and created so much buzz, while others like Sony simply make money? Have you tried to figure out where certain people find the much-needed strength to see their creations become game changers for society? If so, then the Third Circle Theory will elevate your awareness of the reasoning and unlock the mystery behind how some of us become visionaries while others don't.

Understanding how the Third Circle Theory works will help you understand why Michael Jordan, Steve Jobs, Walt Disney, and Thomas Edison will be remembered forever; while the founders of Citigroup, Exxon, and the original owner of the Chicago Bulls basketball team will not be. As you explore the depths of each circle, you will search within your own life and identify why you have been successful so far, or why you haven't been. You will grow even further as a result of your understanding or comprehend the obstacles that have kept you from living your life to your greatest potential.

I need to warn you that the intention of this book is not to change you, but instead empower you to make changes. My goal is to inspire self-reflection and create the awareness you need to know who you are today and why. There may be sections that will evoke emotions, and you might even disagree with what I say. There will also be times when you may want to stop reading, because your values, beliefs, or perspectives may be questioned. Self-realization can be a blessing or a curse, but it is ultimately in your own best interest to see your true image and how others see you in that very same mirror. Since this book is highly focused on the importance of understanding others, then it is only reasonable that you need to identify how others see you and why. As I mentioned earlier, there is no right or wrong, only perspective and information that over time will grow within your mind and heighten your awareness to things that you may have not yet recognized.

By investing in reading the Third Circle Theory, you will learn to adjust your perspective to understand others and experience the reward of being able to define yourself through the observations of others. More importantly, you will understand the critical value of letting go of the self-centric approach you have been accustomed to, and instead move towards a level of selflessness that you may not know existed within yourself.

The Third Circle Theory will take you on a transformational journey opening your mind and your heart to a vast world of opportunity. When you are prepared to move forward toward greater success and a more fulfilled life, turn the page.

Why Do You Exist?

This question is often left unanswered as its meaning can be interpreted in about a thousand ways, yet none as conclusive as we would like. The reason for our existence can be linked to faith, belief, circumstance, and nothing more than destiny. So why do we exist, and why are we all so different from one another? What makes some of us more capable than others? Why do some of us excel at something while others are so much better in other ways? All of these are valid and powerful questions, but none are as important as why we exist.

We must all play a role in a bigger picture, but what role? Is God testing you? Or perhaps faith has left you with the belief that procreation is the ultimate way to leave a legacy behind and create a sense of purpose for yourself. We do, after all, hear many mothers and fathers saying, "I live through my children" or "I wish for you to have what I never had."

Maybe life is not as complicated as we make it out to be. Perhaps it's just about making a lot of money and living happily. Despite all these uncertainties, some concepts are factual and not philosophical at all, such as being influenced by your environment. Each of us at some point or another is a by-product of our environment; and all of us, no matter how hard we work, are a sum of our actions. At some point we have all felt some sort of emotion, and as a result reacted to it in a way we later regretted; thus experiencing different levels of fear that prevented us from doing things we knew would help us move forward in life. Regardless of how much impact this has had on your life, these are the experiences we must go through in order to evolve.

These actions can all be linked, explained, and answered. Then we can identify the reasons why certain people are so much more successful than others. Why do some people achieve the highest level of fulfillment, while so many others find themselves lost in an endless cycle where life just never seems to cut them a break? Does this sound familiar? Where are you in the spectrum?

This "break" or help you seek stems from nothing more than your inability to deal with the situation you are in right now. You lack the acceptance that your life really holds no weight or importance — at least, not yet.

If we accept that all successful individuals share certain traits, we can conclude that some skill set or process exists that delivers a higher rate of success. We can also deduce that although highly successful individuals may not be connected to one another, they share more in common than most.

These individuals share similar experiences and viewpoints towards society that enable them to see and implement innovative ways to change their world. They connect the dots more quickly and can envision the grand scheme of things, not just the narrow view of what they are shown. These visionaries possess passion, determination, and the strong belief that their life's purpose is to bring these innovations to life. Therefore, they live devoted to building on their ideas or projects so that they can eventually change the world as they see fit.

What is it that makes them so special? Why can they do things that you can't? And lastly, did this outcome have anything to do with destiny? Are some of us destined to be more successful than others? Are we here to change humanity or to simply maintain it? Who decides all these things?

Faith versus Opportunity

The discussion of these questions takes us to the faith versus opportunity debate, which you can argue forever. But it doesn't just take religious belief to sometimes concede with "it wasn't meant to be." It's often true that you look for a greater reason for things to happen (or not). You might blame missing an employment opportunity or a big hit on the belief that it must not have been the right deal or just wasn't your time for it. It is difficult to actually accept the fact that perhaps you weren't good enough or not suitably prepared for it.

The same can be said about opportunities that your successful idols and role models took in their lives. Was it their time to shine when all the stars were aligned? Or was there a greater power at work, like destiny or faith? Maybe it was even simpler than that - it was nothing more than hard work.

What made their opportunities more valuable than yours?

Those individuals do not dismiss opportunities. They are prepared for them while you; on the other hand, do not realize that you can actually have more awareness of your surroundings. Instead, you give up and blame faith.

"Opportunities lie all around us, from the lifetime opportunities we encounter everyday by meeting new people and learning from them, to new directions we can take our lives. These opportunities appear in front of us each and every minute that we exist. In most cases we miss most of them, because we are not looking for them and most likely dismiss them."

The easiest way to put this in perspective is to think of an occasion when you wanted something. For instance, when you buy a Mercedes, you will notice them more on the streets even though the number of them hasn't increased. The same goes for other things like the latest electronics or designer clothes.

If you buy a rare purse, you will notice others who also own one, which wouldn't have been the case before you bought it. Opportunities are also included in that mix, but the difference is you actually have to know what specific opportunities you are looking for. In most cases, you haven't yet defined those targets. How can you aim for something when you don't know what or where it is?

Awareness has a lot to do with seeing the right opportunities; seizing that opportunity is the other half of the equation. Grabbing hold relies heavily on your understanding of the opportunity, but you also have to be ready to take action when you encounter it.

Readiness can also be tricky when you aren't clear about what you are seeking. If you can't connect with a golden opportunity when it arises, you might miss your chance. You can blame it on lack of faith or some other factor, but perhaps you should look more closely. Was it really faith or lack of faith in yourself that let the opportunity pass you by?

Success can be defined as hard work meets opportunity, but opportunity is a very broad word. Even where hard work exists, opportunity may seem like it never appeared. In reality, you didn't know what to look for. If you are not prepared, the action or lack of action might appear as though you lack confidence or ability to get the job done. So that opportunity you missed is presented to the people that you believe had the luck to be blessed with faith or belief — and that's why you think they succeeded.

In truth, their purpose wasn't revealed to them through faith or even a dream, and certainly their vision didn't come to them by a biblical figure. It was nothing more than a combination of their past experiences, amplified by their ability to see further and deeper than others, which also came from their hard work and belief in themselves.

How does confidence play a role in finding purpose? Confidence is accumulated through experiences you go through over the years, and certainly is a very important part of finding your purpose. If you lack confidence, you probably won't discover the power to identify why you exist. Doubt and purpose have no relation in this equation.

Let's be clear here. Don't confuse confidence with arrogance. Yes, they are a hairline's distance apart, but they are still two distinct attitudes and traits that differentiate your abilities.

Confidence is self-belief based on tenure or track record, which ultimately is the brain's way of self-acknowledgment in a field or perhaps of a skill set.

Arrogance, on the other hand, is a highly manipulative trait where a person believes himself to be superior to others without any real merit or accomplishments to support it.

Despite being similar, the two traits are very different and are not mistaken for each other by highly confident individuals. Individuals who lack self-confidence will mistake the two, and as a result call confident people "cocky," "arrogant," or "stuck up." True confidence is needed in order to initiate the hard work that is based on vision, which ultimately allows your purpose to manifest itself. More importantly, confidence originates from experiences and is much more related to purpose than you currently think. For now, simply understand that without confidence you're unlikely to identify or realize what your life's purpose is.

Now, when can you identify your life's purpose? Your view of the world changes with time, age, and your experiences. We are ultimately the by-products of our environments (I will later prove to you why that is true no matter what your current point of view is).

These environments, which are ever changing and based on the decisions and choices you make, evoke a new side or skill set within you. They enable you to adapt, which may prompt you to change your perspective.

Think of when you lived somewhere for a long time and then moved. The new place seems so strange at first, but with time you will adapt. The old place will no longer seem the same when you visit it again. This change of perspective is attributed to experiencing another life, which you were previously unaware existed. Components of this new life have become part of your perspective, vision, and mindset. With this new information, what you saw or knew before has been altered.

With time and experiences altering your perspective, your fields of understanding and vision change too. The same can be applied to identifying opportunities. If you look at a computer at an early age, you might only see it as a vehicle for playing video games. As you grow older, you discover many more uses for the computer. Your needs grow as you do. You buy more software or upgrade your equipment. You might decide to learn about coding, and then design the software yourself instead of buying it. As a result, you create an opportunity for yourself to sell or trademark the program. The same item, which had been used to play video games, has now made you a millionaire; and it was nothing more than information and perspective that allowed you to identify a different use and purpose.

At every turning point of your life, you discover life's objectives. Your discoveries are based on how much you see, which is tied to how much previous information you received. This either makes it an opportunity or just entertainment.

Purpose can be identified only when you:

• See the world correctly (Awareness)
• Hold enough information, and
• Confidence to act on discovering more

As a result, you will feel purposeful—even if you have yet to discover your life's purpose. At different stages of your life, you might feel like you hold multiple purposes as you identify your objectives. But it is often later when all your experiences and your past feelings of fulfillment come together, which ultimately allow you to reach a level of true self-actualization.

Is your job today relevant to finding your purpose tomorrow? Absolutely. You most likely chose the role you hold today, and regardless of whether or not you are passionate about it; your job holds certain elements of what you are meant to do in the long run. For myself, I started in the finance industry at a relatively young age and evolved into multiple leadership roles there. Despite hating the job itself or those I worked for, I enjoyed the way I helped employees grow and discover their paths in life. It was invigorating to see them succeed and feel like I played a part in that. Later in life, I found that I possessed a great skill set to help people in this way. I also understood that my unique life experiences enabled me to help them more than most, so I asked myself how I could help more people which led me down a new path — which I believe is the reason I exist. I also wish it to be the reason why my existence is validated by society.

Without having had jobs I hated, I wouldn't have identified all the elements that were missing; and without experiences from my past, I wouldn't have been able to act on them. Think about the common factor that you didn't like about all your past jobs: what is that one missing element?

The roles you hold today or have held in the past are linked to what you will do later, but perhaps not in ways that you might identify immediately or even relate to. You can; however, back track once you understand the Third Circle Theory and identify for yourself why you work where you work and why you worked at previous jobs.

More importantly, you will identify elements in your skill sets or beliefs that all your past roles had in common at that time. Take a moment and think back to all your past jobs and the positions you held. What were the common responsibilities you enjoyed in your roles?

By understanding and applying the Third Circle Theory, you can identify what to do today to help position what you see tomorrow and remain on track to discover your true life's purpose.

How the Third Circle Theory Will Help You

Purpose is often defined through mystery, luck, or faith. I've never had it explained through a systematic lens of life's cycles in a way that provides a pattern, process, or something more tangible than those other pathways.

Success is defined differently for each individual, but the road to success, regardless of your definition, shares a lot of the same attributes. One example is consistency being an attribute of success. I expect that anyone who has succeeded in life will tell you that consistency in one way or another played a role in their quest. The same pattern of consistency is how most people found what they believe to be their purpose in life. They experienced a number of common experiences such as surrounding themselves with role models or being raised by people other than their real parents, which led them to who and where they are today.

The Third Circle Theory is a road map; the steps we take in life, experiences we go through, and the surroundings we observe are all part of this theory. It shows you how to navigate life—progressing from one circle to the next—ultimately discovering your true passion and leading to what you are meant to do.

Why the Third Circle Theory Was Created

Something was always different for me when I was growing up. I saw most of life through a weird third-party lens, like a spectator. From a very young age, I was able to be logical and emotionless towards situations. With this purely rational perspective, I observed my surroundings and those in it, while never really understanding at the time how everything and everyone was interconnected.

What was most interesting was that no matter what I started—like getting an education or a nice job—I never really found fulfillment, just temporary satisfaction. I bought new cars, homes, and luxury gadgets that many people dream of, but I got bored with them in a few months. I dated beautiful women, but became just as bored with them and moved on.

But there was one constant thing that didn't bore me: the knowledge I gained from each experience. No matter what the experience was, I immediately absorbed knowledge. I discovered that I had a natural talent for sharing that knowledge in a charismatic and profound way—one that inspired others to act. With each person I helped or touched during my corporate career, I became more and more motivated; and I was full of energy to do it all over again.

At first, I believed that I had found my purpose, and it was helping others succeed at what they did, but I was wrong. I had not uncovered my purpose, but instead what I was passionate about. This discovery led me to become even more analytical with myself and look back at all my experiences, so that I could understand what my purpose really was.

I realized through this experience that every time I helped someone who worked for me succeed, it held a residual effect for me. As their supervisor, their efforts directly benefited me, so I knew something was keeping me from taking the next step towards finding my purpose.

I asked myself over and over: how was I actually helping people? Was it by changing their mindset? Was it motivation? Or perhaps it was nothing more than offering them a logical approach rather than an emotional one. I really couldn't differentiate what it was exactly that I was doing to help them, or in what order. I knew I was helping them as their results proved that my method worked, even though it wasn't much of a method, but different components of different things all coming together through my words and presented in a way that everyone would buy into it.

I didn't know what I triggered in them to make them change and didn't understand how my techniques worked for everyone, but I certainly knew why it was very important for me to continue helping others—ultimately helping society all together by introducing smarter and brighter people each and every day. I kept helping and in various ways continued to see results.

Time after time, my methods worked as planned until the one day I ran into failure. Ten years of positive results had passed when I finally met the exception to my rules. No matter what I said or how I said it, she didn't believe me, didn't change, and didn't improve. My method failed with this young lady. As shocked as I was, I actually enjoyed analyzing why I failed and attempted to find out from her why she never trusted me. She responded, "Because I thought you wanted to help me so you could use me to get yourself ahead." Despite being hurt, shocked, and puzzled as to why she would feel that way, I understood that I simply hadn't earned enough trust for her to believe me.

I tackled the situation in my usual unemotional, analytical way. I evaluated why others trusted me while she didn't. For example, I broke down the different segments of what I did with others that I didn't do with her.

After careful study, I finally came to realize that it wasn't what I did or didn't do with her, but rather what was done or not done to her prior to meeting me. Her past environment taught her to not trust those who want to help. She had been conditioned to believe these people would most likely be using you. This discovery made me realize that "environment" plays a much more significant role in someone's growth. More importantly, it also made me have to rethink my own environment and how it had altered my thinking through the years. That's when I realized that what I was teaching everyone was just a combination of my learning. I also discovered that how I was teaching them was almost identical to how I learned. However, the reason why I was teaching them was because I wanted them to know what it's like to find their purpose, what it's like to feel like you understand your role in this world, and the importance it holds.

I created the Third Circle Theory as a result of my experiences, because I believe more people need to discover for themselves why they are here. More importantly, they need to see and experience more of life, understand what living is, and start becoming less selfish and more driven to help one another.

The Third Circle Theory will help you identify what you must do to find your purpose. The circles themselves help identify various elements in your environment and the roles they play in your quest. Many of the actions you take or watch others go through are defined in these circles. Hopefully, this direction will help you identify and connect the dots to what you must change to get to that Third Circle.

Before we start, let's analyze something that might make you open your mind a bit more to the concept of change itself. Let's talk about common sense.

What is common sense, and where does it come from? Common sense is often represented as something that must be understood by most as the mini skill set to survive in society.

It is your ability to connect the dots and make sense of life's most common theories. In the simplest terms, it is how we live. Those who don't "get it" are labeled as lacking "street smarts" or as idiots.

True common sense; however, is more than just how we live. It goes a bit deeper than someone categorizing you into one group or another. Common sense is the majority of the group (country, city, organization, etc.) agreeing on certain beliefs or values. In this way, they come to a common agreement that whatever is discussed to be true. So if a common group believes in a system based on colors and concludes that red means stop and green means go, they introduce this belief to a common group as an agreed upon concept. It now becomes a commonly accepted symbol of that group or society. Anyone not conforming would be deemed as lacking common sense. This common belief had to be created somewhere and by someone. Therefore, it may or may not be true, but the group now accepts it. If other groups don't accept this theory, then they create their own commonly accepted rules or symbols. In return, they will naturally create a disconnect if one party from each group spends a day with the other party. This is no different than what society goes through as immigrants of one country with X amount of beliefs comes into Y country with different sets of rules and beliefs. Most of their actions in their new environment will mimic the actions they observed for the years they spent in their past environment, creating confusion among others who will quickly call them stupid or say they "don't get it," but perhaps the tables would be turned if you visited a new country or place.

The real question though is why is your group's set of values and beliefs more accurate than others? Who decides which group is right or wrong, and which sets of values and beliefs are indeed accurate?

Since you now recognize that common sense is nothing more than your very own observed beliefs, you can understand why the world has so many different individuals at so many different levels of understanding. We can tie it all into the Third Circle Theory.

Third Circle Theory Introduction

I created the Third Circle Theory for Secret Entourage, a platform aimed at helping the rebirth of entrepreneurship, to explain how the human mind evolves from birth to the stage where it finds purpose. This theory cannot only help you realize why you are not finding your purpose, but can actually guide you in the right direction to find it.

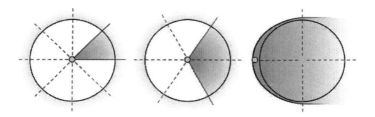

The Third Circle Theory consists of three circles illustrating three worlds, three perspectives, three visions, and three cycles.

Each circle consists of:

• A world

• A perspective

• A vision

• A cycle

Your mind undergoes each of these four elements. Each circle represents a path you can take. Through time, you can evolve from one to the next. You do not have to complete a circle in order to graduate to the next circle.

Everyone goes through the First Circle, some will evolve to the Second Circle, and very few progress to the Third Circle, which is the stage that allows the definition of your existence. My hope is that by reading this book, you will join that elite group of purposeful people.

The First Circle: The Birth, The Settler, & The Dreamer

Everyone begins in the First Circle. It is the foundation of your life, and regardless of how strong that foundation is, you begin here.

The Birth: Signifies that you are born into this circle.

As a child the world revolves around you, which is the significance of the diagram's center dot. You are a product of the environment you are born into and the practices you are taught early on. Your religious habits, beliefs, values, and behaviors are all derived from someone else's perspective of life, often a parent. Your value system, views, and reach extend only as far as theirs. You strive for the things you are exposed to. For example, if you are from a family that struggles to make ends meet or raised in sickness or with issues, you could find yourself more exposed to individuals with little hope for something better as well as a significant amount of faith or belief in things that are uncontrollable. As a result, you strive to rise above poverty or to gain better health as your main goal.

Your aspirations at this stage also remain small, perhaps because your family's goals for you are equally as small as their own were. This is where they tell you about opportunities they never had, and that unlike them, you will make a difference by acquiring an education. **They might blame you for their own failures and make an example of what they sacrificed in order to bring you to this world.** But you need to put this into perspective. If you are blamed, it is mostly because your parents (or caregivers) never themselves graduated from this First Circle, so they are stuck in a narrow-minded enclosure.

On the contrary, if you are born into a family where neither money nor accomplishments are scarce, you too will strive to do great things. The exposure to this more optimistic lifestyle reinforces your belief of what success is, what you can achieve, and what you deserve. This is where the idea of entitlement starts. Entitled or not, in this environment, you are always exposed to what you can be. Not only is support available for you to achieve your goals; but resources, belief, and constant encouragement also exist. While education and the core foundation may not differ much from being born into poverty, the constant level of achievement present all around you forces you out of this First Circle much faster, propelling you toward finding what you are meant to do.

Remember that from an early stage you are born with or without an advantage, but by no means are you obligated to accept the outcome you are born into. You simply have to endure it.

The Settler: An individual stage that represents being complacent in your situation.

Most who continue on from the Birth stage to the Settler have achieved just enough to be satisfied. In most cases, you would not have seen much of what life has to offer. You feel that the little you have achieved is the big achievement of your life.

At this stage, life and the world revolve around you. It's about your work, your relationships, your money, and your feelings. Routine sets in. Most of your earlier beliefs, behaviors, and faith are followed and maintained with direction from those above you—your elders, supervisors, or wealthier individuals are highly respected without question. You are simply happy and deal with life's cycles and different stages, which are represented by all the alternative

28

viewpoints (dotted lines). They are all very narrow and only an alternate view of the main vision, which is equally narrow (illustrated by the bold line).

Your viewpoint can only see so far and is limited to what you are shown, since at any given time, you miss what is occurring in alternative views, times, and locations around you. By staying in the Settler stage, your mind accepts its inability to grow and settles for whatever it has achieved to date. While you will catch a few breaks here and there, you will ultimately never really progress.

In the Settler stage, you will showcase traits like disinterest towards what goes on in the world. You will be apathetic about voting of any sort, but will be sold on just about anything commercial. Most of today's TV commercials are geared to this state of the mind: one that is easily convinced by what it is exposed to.

The Dreamer: The stage where dreams and reality never meet.

Due to your Settler viewpoint, you have become complacent. You move on to a mid-life stage. If you have not graduated from the First Circle, you go into a "mid-life crisis," which is your brain's way of seeking a better reality than you ever had. As you get older, you are exposed to new individuals—many older and many much more successful, which makes you question your past decision-making. As a result, you want to belong to something you are not. Since you are way into your life cycle, your brain continuously looks for ways to catch up and therefore, is always hungry for a quick answer. This need for instant gratification creates what we call the "Dreamer."

In this stage, you now analyze the lives of your friends or others. Their gains and progress unfortunately feels out of your reach so you become very bitter and blame your family or some other form of faith. You go back to your Settler state once you acquire something like a new car or larger home—

vanities that please the weaker side of your mind into feeling accomplished when no real change has occurred.

This period often ends, and very little has happened. Your mind failed at expanding itself and moving forward. The dreamer stage also indicates why Gen Y is highly focused on instant gratification. If you fit into this vision, you find yourself easily manipulated by scams or by false opportunities as you are seeking shortcuts and answers to becoming something you spend a long time ignoring. This constant pursuit of instant gratification in this stage is the reason that very profitable self-help programs target individuals at the Dreamer stage. Rich Dad, Poor Dad is highly geared to "dads" who are often in their 40's and haven't accomplished what they wanted—the consummate Dreamers.

Unfortunately, most people never graduate from the First Circle. While they are followers who seem lost to others who have graduated, they still can make the transition at any time. The real problem is that if you stay in the First Circle, you will remain set in your ways, which is difficult to change. This is the reason why many young adults feel that their parents don't understand their aspirations when they think differently than a conventional way to succeed. The real change from the previous generation (Gen X) to Gen Y as it pertains to the First Circle is the time it takes to move through the stages. Gen Y will simply go through the phases of each circle faster due to the widely available amount of information. The access to information is good and bad. Information, if accurate, is great as it allows you to make a conclusion based on facts, but today's society shares opinions based on perspectives that will differ depending on the source of information. This creates serious mass confusion and often manipulation to a level unheard of before.

The characteristics lacking in most people in the First Circle are based around self-perception. Most of the individuals here lack self-confidence, courage, and belief in themselves partly because they have poor perception of the world and where they fit in it. They don't feel significant enough to accomplish anything, often not even knowing what they want to do in life. They stay complacent with their environment, don't take chances, don't start businesses, don't travel as much to places they haven't been to before, and are good with anything that happens. They are often drawn to individuals who, unlike themselves, seem to have all the answers, which is why the First Circle people are easily manipulated. They often perceive others as arrogant instead of confident, as they are unable to identify confidence and what it does for one's body and mind.

The Second Circle: The Awakening, The Leader, & The Achiever

About 20 percent of you will progress to this stage, either naturally or through exposure to knowledge followed by curiosity. The Second Circle reflects The Awakening, The Leader, and The Achiever.

At some point during your life cycle, you are exposed to individuals, education, or points of view that defy your beliefs, faith, and behaviors as explained in the First Circle. You have the opportunity to graduate to the Second Circle, which consists of an increased perspective, vision, and view of the world. These broadened views empower your thinking to grow even further. The Second Circle is about your openness to expanding your mind and vision, beginning with the first stage.

The Awakening: Your mind opens up to heightened awareness and curiosity.

When you are exposed to the unknown, you either choose to accept that an alternative reality exists or you simply deny your brain access to freethinking. Often, again based on your previous beliefs, this decision is presented to you in different ways throughout your lifetime. A significant portion of that comes from education, as you are not only faced with new learning, but are also forced to accept the message in order to graduate to become an accepted member of society.

Through this exposure to new ways of thinking, you are challenged to seek your own answers and deliver your opinions, which makes you question your narrow view of society. This is often why people who go to better schools end up in better jobs, simply because of their exposure to people who operate in this Second Circle. This Awakening makes you curious enough to try new things, seek new answers, and even make you skeptical at times. It inspires you to explore, and through exploration comes learning, regardless of whether it came from an educator, mentor, or teacher.

You learn to think freely and start realizing that, despite the world still being centered on yourself and your emotions and needs, it is also up to you to reach for your goals. The awakening of your mind allows you to gain courage and confidence—enough to get you to pursue your interests instead of merely doing as you are told. Being in the Awakening stage almost makes you defiant to society. You might start to believe in conspiracies and notice that everything appears to have a double meaning due to your lack of trust towards information.

In the Awakening, you may lose significant trust as you believe you have lived a life that has been filled with fabrication. Being cautious in this stage is important for your well being, because there are people with a deep understanding of the fact that you seek answers and they are ready to manipulate you. The power of manipulation continues as ideologies are shared and answers to questions are provided, creating a false sense of trust because you relate to a cause or person sharing it. In other words, your brain is awakening to a new world, and this new influence becomes a guide. If an individual misguides you, they are likely manipulating you for their own self-interest. This realization takes us to that next stage.

The Leader: The emerging need and desire to lead others.

If you are able to overcome other opinions and beliefs that are attempting to sway your thinking in the Awakening stage, you'll feel unrest and distrust. You believe that you are in charge of your outcomes and feel the need to share that confidence with others. Through your actions, you become successful and build a following of employees, peers, or supporters who revolve around catering to your needs. **This necessity of leading others benefits those around you by providing them their needs while getting you what you want.**

Others are drawn to your character, which amplifies your ability to grow even further and become even more efficient and effective as a leader. If you are in the Leader stage, you are often looked at as a very successful and leading person in you fields of interest. You establish yourself with a high level of education whether it was self-taught or through school. More importantly, you keep relating back to a series of experiences as the reason for your success when sharing with others how you have become so resourceful.

This stage is easy to lose yourself in, as you are a self-proclaimed leader. As a result, you may find yourself making a good amount of money, slowly closing your eyes to further learning. This dangerous path is the beginning stage where you can show manipulation traits, such as looking for ways to profit off of those admiring you and looking to you for advice. These traits may be amplified by your self-acceptance and your group of followers increasing faster than you expect. As a result of being a leader and open to viewing multiple points of view, you become more wary of your environment. You may also become an opportunist in good or poor manners, either manipulating your environment to benefit yourself versus those following you looking for guidance. You then evolve to the third stage of this circle.

The Achiever: Opportunity meets hard work.

People in this stage of the Second Circle are no strangers to the concept of hard work and opportunity. You deliver daily on your new self-created belief and see other's weaknesses as an opportunity to step up and lead them. Self-proclaimed and profit-driven self-help gurus often live in this phase.

As an Achiever, you aim to be accepted in society, and therefore constantly seek answers to why you exist. This quest leads you to multiple paths, all successful and all full of achievements (illustrated through multiple dotted lines showing only four stages, but still multiple stages of one's life). Most people in this stage are still highly focused on money as the ideal reward for their efforts. You rarely seek fulfillment unless monetarily rewarded for it. If you look at the graph, it showcases a higher and broader view, but still keeps the self-centered individual from seeing more of life. Therefore, **if unable to graduate from this Second Circle, you will be accomplished but never define your existence.**

Most of today's top lawyers, doctors, and businessmen fall into the Achiever category. While you do succeed, instead of graduating to the Third Circle, you work your entire life to make more money as your way to keep score. Very few of you actually feel you know your purpose—even if you believe you do, it is only to convince yourself that you have found it. The power of self-acceptance is very strong in the Achiever. This stage also amplifies the manipulative side of people in it, constantly using resources for self-benefit and leading people on to promises that never become reality. However, if you determine that your existence should and will mean more than money, then you graduate to the Third Circle where you find the answers you seek. This takes us to the Third Circle and to the core of why you exist.

The Third Circle: The Vision, The Purpose, & The Rebirth

The Third Circle is the one that people most often miss. As a matter of fact, only about two percent of people fall into that Third Circle (or better said, graduate into the Third Circle). People whose achievements we idolize, such as Steve Jobs, Bill Gates, Michael Jordan, Walt Disney, Elon Musk, Gandhi, and many more whom we remember despite their departure from this world, lived their lives the way this circle intended. You listen to their words, idolize their lives, look to them for answers, and consider them to be the best in their respective industries. These individuals are not god-like but have figured out something that many of you will never accept, which will prevent you from entering this circle. They have learned their purpose and how to remove themselves from the equation of life.

When you reach a satisfactory level of achievement in the Second Circle, you will start to question your existence as the human mind has been conditioned to seek more. After all, it is the "Achiever" in you. It isn't until you choose to not make it about you that you establish a true vision of what the world can be. This allows you to graduate into the Third Circle, starting with your vision.

Since the Third Circle Theory is not about you, the stages are reversed. Starting with the Vision, then moving to the Purpose, and finally to the Rebirth of you. The Circle itself is yet another stage of your life. It is your ability to go past this Circle and enhance your perspective to one that does not see yourself as the center of the universe, but instead as one removed from the universe. That will give you the ability to identify your purpose. The diagram of the Third Circle indicates the vision being outside of the Circle to showcase this entire view of the world at once from a much broader perspective.

> **The Vision**: Envision a better world or see past your own emotions.

Some traits of the Second Circle's Visionary exist in many of you, but your inability to see that every situation or problem isn't about you prevents you from finding your purpose.

When you reach the Visionary stage in the Third Circle, you are keenly aware of your surroundings and very analytical of the information presented to you. You see what you are not shown or told, rather than what is presented. A great example of this is looking into a cell phone screen: many of you see the image itself, while other people see their own reflection. It is not because you have better eyesight, but because you seek alternative answers all around you; and therefore, you can see farther than most. You envision a better world, a better future for people, and you can actually picture what that looks like. This vision enables you to apply importance to your project; no matter how big or small it may seem to others at times.

Because you see farther, you do not fear bringing that vision to life or the work ahead of you. A world without that vision is no longer possible once you have seen it. Realizing that image becomes your obsession. Some of you are often referred to as philosophers. The graph here illustrates the view from outside of the circle, showcasing an entire projection of the world rather than multiple segments at different times. The Vision grows stronger than your own being. The wheels start rolling, and your desire to bring the vision to life becomes your priority, which leads to defining your purpose.

The Purpose: Choose which side of the equation you stand on.

Almost a clash of good versus evil, you can choose what you want the world to look like. If you choose that the world remains unchanged about you, you ultimately choose to take the wrong side of life and become an amazing manipulator. You can start showing traits of this early on like we discussed in the Second Circle where you chose how you handled people who were followers or believers of you and your cause. But like any other human going through the stages, you have the opportunity to change. Those who choose not to maximize opportunity don't progress past the Third Circle.

At this time in your life, whichever side you choose is the side you will remain with and is complementary to your vision. Purpose is created as a result of your belief in something greater than yourself, where you allow your mind and emotions to remove themselves from the equation. This is the stage in which money no longer matters, and decisions are made for the common good of the vision rather than your desires, needs, and wants.

The feeling of belonging to something greater sets in and can be very contagious. Those around you often feel this energy and passion and jump on the bandwagon to share that same positive feeling.

The experiences from the first two circles all play into your purpose, and connecting the dots to life's concepts becomes an easier task for you. The grand scheme of life reveals itself, and your existence can only be validated when your vision comes to life. This means that your existence is null, and your feelings are ignored until the bigger picture becomes reality. A high level of energy reveals itself, allowing no obstacles or problems, and serving up challenges that always have answers that are quickly overcome. This is outlined by the dot outside the circle, which is a symbol that the world no longer revolves around you, but instead in front of you.

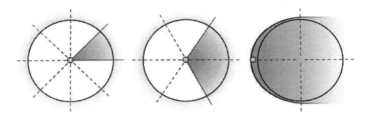

Decision-making becomes easier. The project at hand or those involved become more important than you. You are now feeling fulfillment—the driving force that you must support others and help them achieve in order to reach the goal. Here, a new level of leader is born within you and the Rebirth occurs.

The Rebirth: Your mind frees itself of the unknown and instead focuses on the newly established vision.

Your rebirth occurs when your vision is recognized by all, and not just those around you. With this recognized level of achievement comes an immense boost of confidence, and your mind seeks new ways to advance society.

Ultimately, it will never soar as high as the first time, because your existence was never acknowledged to begin with when you were going through the three circles. As a result, you created the need to work harder than ever before; you had never felt a feeling of purpose and as a result pushed to find it. Many of you in The Rebirth stage become speakers, teachers, and public servants who bring their knowledge and self- awareness to good use. The mind is free, the vision established, and the purpose defined and recognized. **The game of life has been mastered**.

The Rebirth can be a tricky stage; you might feel you have reached this point by skipping other steps. Politicians, athletes, and celebrities are examples because even though their existence is recognized, it's only for a short duration as money can give a false sense of power. Only those individuals who become legendary will end up establishing their purpose as entertainers, icons, or role models.

When money is introduced early on—such as when a large inheritance is left behind for a child —the same theory applies. However, the order of the Third Circle's stages will shift as the Achiever stage was never reached, but instead created with experiences. This shift makes it difficult for anyone to realize the importance of removing themselves from the equation.

Other misinterpretations of the Third Circle are those visionaries who see the world from the correct lens, but remain self-centered. These people choose to ignore others instead of helping change their lives. As opposed to becoming innovators or game changers, these individuals become powerful manipulators and con artists who alter perception to their advantage. Be advised that there is no alternate route to Rebirth. Selflessness and the Vision must take place in the right order and for the right reasons in order to create the true sense of your purpose.

The Third Circle Theory can be applied to just about any level of thinking, from leadership, management, faith, and more importantly, to entrepreneurship. The Circles hold the key to finding your purpose in today's complex society.

The Third Circle Theory allows you to see why powerful people like Steve Jobs don't just make computers, but they rewrite history. Any one of you can advance from one Circle to another and eventually reach a new level of thinking where purpose and existence are validated. But it is often your desire to skip ahead and grab all the answers without the hard work and experiences that keeps you grounded in the first Circle. Think of the people you know who talk about businesses and ideas, yet never act on them. They are all Dreamers, and because they feel entitled they never do the work to achieve real progress. How many people give up on their businesses because they didn't make enough money? That is a self-centered approach to the idea of success - they never achieve innovation and affect real change in an industry.

By applying the **Third Circle Theory, you have the power to understand why you do what you do and why you can or cannot progress**. It also explains why you see what you see and what you must observe to allow your mind to expand. If it is understood and applied to any phase of life, this theory can help you take the journey to finding your purpose.

Now that you understand why it's important, and what it is: take it one step further. Look at how the Third Circle Theory works and how you can use it to advance yourself through the circles and find your purpose.

Progression of The Mind

Now that you understand what the three Circles mean, you are ready to explore the cycles within each Circle. In so doing, you will learn how to transition from one to the next, while understanding why people progress slower or faster than others.

As I said earlier, the Circles are driven and navigated by what you observe, which impacts how you think. Therefore, your awareness of the information you are receiving is the first step to understanding the Circles. Awareness is the single most important and often neglected aspect of your life. You take so many things around you for granted by not investigating the information. Take this book, for example. The fact that you are aware of the information you've read here now enables you to look for the signs that validate it. In other words, you are now subconsciously looking for your purpose, which means that even if you put this book down right now, you already know that finding your purpose is based on what you see and the environments around you. Whether or not you believe this information at this moment changes nothing at all, because you are **aware** of this possibility.

Your mind is open to accept further information that clarifies beliefs to be true or false. Prior to reading about the Third Circle Theory, you may not have been open to these possibilities. Investigating this information is what enables you to move through the Circles faster than others. When you are able to accept alternate realities faster, you work towards your own truth immediately rather than waiting for clarification. Once again, your ability to act rather than not do anything is the key to succeeding.

The First Circle

In the next few sections, I will break down the traits, observations, and segments that will enable you to move through the three Circles. Each Circle has its own set of components. The farther you go, the less the components matter and the more your actions towards them will.

Keep in mind that most of you already possess or have mastered some of these components. You need to follow this guide to apply some order and connect the dots so that you can fill in any missing pieces. You can sometimes complete the big picture of your own life by understanding which pieces of each Circle you have yet to master. Let's get started with the First Circle.

The First Circle encompasses the Birth, the Settler, and the Dreamer; it is the one we are all born into. Although we all start here, we won't each stay in this Circle for the same amount of time. The pace you move beyond this Circle depends on how quickly you master the following eight segments of your life.

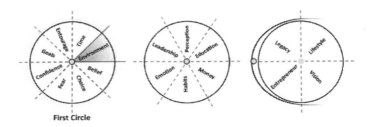

First Circle

Environment

From birth, we are each a by-product of our environment. Infants have no choice as to what circumstance they are born into. Regardless of what class, religion, ethnicity, race, place, or education level we are born into, we absorb the environment. As children, we don't make a conscious choice of language or religion. We don't have a say in likes or dislikes, but we do have a set of eyes that are constantly seeing and analyzing what is around us. We derive our determination of right versus wrong from what we observe in our early years. We often try to imitate what we see more than from what is said. We build trust through consistency and use that as a foundation for the way we should act. Altogether, these create what we consider our set of values — consisting of behaviors we have witnessed from early childhood to early teenage years. These values become our guiding principles, and it is very difficult for someone to make us believe that they are wrong or that an alternate set of values exists.

A great example of this is the controversial topic of religion. Regardless of what you believe, all religions are founded on the belief in something greater than yourself. Think about your own religion — not God, just the concept of religion. Ask yourself who chose your religion. Were you given an opportunity to learn or try other religions besides that of your parents or family? Did you have the opportunity to interact with individuals of other religions? In most cases, you are the same religion as your parents, guardians, or those around you — and most likely still are. That's fine, as long as you understand why.

You are the sum of your values, beliefs, and the environments you absorb. Religion and faith are constants that you witness from a very young age and maybe are forced to follow by your parents. This situation puts you at a disadvantage from birth, not because religion is wrong, but because you are taught to not question certain things. You are taught that authority shouldn't be questioned, and that information from certain sources such as your church must always be deemed accurate. On the other hand, imagine that you do not have religion in your upbringing. Perhaps it was not discussed or practiced in your home. Your lack of awareness and knowledge of it creates a sense of separation from the topic. You become less likely to find religion at all in your life. While some might feel the absence of religion is a terrible thing, it may actually help put individuals ahead of those people who were born into households of religion. Allowing a mind to grow without such boundaries creates very different outcomes. You learn to rely on your own actions.

This can, of course, backfire if the environment you are born into is missing other more important values — those that define your humanity like being polite, respectful, and maintaining empowering principles such as working hard and doing good for others. These are not of religious descents but are preached as good qualities.

In addition to the example of your religious environment, you can look at your parents' habits, the locations where you grew up, the financial status that surrounded you, and even the relationship your parents had with each other and with your siblings. Those external factors drive much of what you do today, often without you even being aware of it. The idea is not to make you question your faith, but why it is the one you practice. You can't answer with "because I believe…" **because belief is emotional, not factual.**

Your environment and the place where you grew up greatly impacts where and how you end up. Think once again about your basic observations as a child. Children don't necessarily listen to the words of their parents, but will imitate them. They are observing their behaviors and increasing their awareness to behaviors. You will likely imitate the behaviors you witnessed as a child — whether they were in a pleasant environment full of cheerfulness, or in a dangerous environment full of violence, fighting, and misery. This environment determines whether you start your journey in life with an advantage or disadvantage. In most cases, you might link these behaviors to money, but it is highly inaccurate to assume that if you were born with wealth then you are most likely to succeed, or if you were born without money then you are more likely to remain poor. It is true that people born with more money have an advantage, but it is because of the behaviors and values that come from individuals who have figured out how to succeed. When you have learned how to succeed, you have better habits and behaviors, and your lifestyle reflects it. As a result, you act within the confines of what society accepts as being successful. Because of that, your focus around making money is not as urgent as those with less money.

Your observations in the environment stage are centered on love, family, healthy eating, exercise, care for your valuables, education, and going to work happy with your job. These behaviors create a good baseline of what you accept your life to be. You don't place as much emphasis on making money, because you feel that you must belong to the environment in which you grew up and carry it on.

This belief is often the reason that many teenagers who are born into wealthier families choose professions that involve a high level of education. This choice is aided by the lack of urgency to make money and because the belief that advanced education is something they witnessed while growing up. Although these individuals have a financial advantage, they are also at a disadvantage. They are so bound by the expectations of their parents that they become consumed with fear of disappointing them.

Let's shift the perspective now and look at the same scenario based on low-income families. In this case, the child witnesses more struggle, stress, and frustration, and even perhaps more violence. But more importantly, witnesses the constant pursuit of basic comforts like money and shelter. This hard-knocks quest paints an image of the importance of money, which is where you become hungry for money as you grow older. You want to compensate for the sacrifices and erase the financial arguments from your memories. Maybe you don't do as well in school, because you think you have alternative options in making money rather than learning. You're applying your intelligence in other ways than formal education.

Even though you are not as likely to succeed in education as the more advantaged person, you thrive in your urgency to make money. You are more likely to venture into the unknown and try new things or be fearless of going after what you want, which once again despite having its downfalls, will hold some type of positive leverage on your growth. This urgency also makes you more vulnerable to get-rich-quick schemes.

What you observe as a child — no matter what side of the equation you are born into — is only a baseline for behaviors and beliefs you inherit, not a final determination of how far you can go. Many additional factors contribute to determining your future long before you even comprehend what you are working towards. The schools you attend, the teachers you have, and certainly the friends you make all impact how you grow up, who you become, and what you achieve. Parents focus on giving the best they can to their children; often based on most expensive or highest rated rather than getting to know the teachers themselves, which ultimately makes the greatest difference in a child's education. This desire to allow children to witness the "right" behaviors and be among others like them is how parents subconsciously help or hurt their kids. This pattern trains the mind to only see one perspective, which is usually why poor teenagers cannot relate to rich teenagers and vice versa. It is because of such parental shelter that a child remains ignorant of what the other side looks like.

Being aware that the environment of your youth is the not the one you chose but was chosen for you is the first step to graduating to a stage of control. You no longer allow your environment to decide your future. Awareness is once again where things begin. Your ability to accept that your parents or past influences are by-products of their environment should allow you to dismiss the idea that all of your learning was factual. Instead, it is a combination of what you observed and the fact that your viewpoint was and still is limited, never allowing you to see more of the world and only accepting the world you are shown.

Now that you understand how your vision has been altered based on what you were shown, what can you do to change it? What can you do to get past the idea of being nothing more than a by-product of your environment?

Awareness is ultimately the answer to everything here, but it is important to understand what you should be aware of. You are already aware of the environment you grew up in and the surroundings you are exposed to everyday, but what about all the other environments you don't have to deal with? Do you actually understand them? Do you truly know how poor people live or how very wealthy people live? Are you aware of their environments and how they act each and every day to move forward? By understanding other people's perspectives you are able to truly comprehend why people think the way they do, and you are able to understand how to manipulate your environment instead of being manipulated by it.

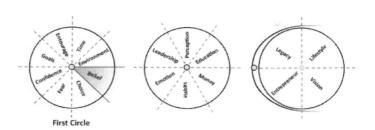

First Circle

Belief

Belief is the second category within the First Circle. Belief is the acceptance of what you see. It's the simplest yet most complex phenomenon due to the fact that your beliefs are engraved for years in yourself and are hard to change. Belief ultimately sums everything up as what you believe in.

What you believe defines what you see as possible, and therefore, becomes your guideline to living life. Belief can be in the sense of what you perceive as right versus wrong or something along the lines of your definition of success.

Belief shouldn't be confused with confidence, which is the belief in your own ability. Belief is defining what you believe to be possible. Yes, it seems similar to confidence, but the true meanings are still very far apart.

Awareness and understanding of your environment leads to your acceptance of it. Think about this in a simpler state— for example, your belief in getting promoted at work. Some people don't believe a promotion is possible, so they never make an effort toward achieving it. It becomes a self-fulfilling prophecy. Lack of belief crushes the chance to achieve.

Others believe in the possibility. They don't just act, but instead seek information to accomplish the task or reach the goal. Then with a plan in mind, they follow through with the actions. It all starts with the belief itself that drives the behavior of investigation.

Your acceptance of what is possible is based on the past observations of your environment. This belief drives you to act. **Your life is only defined by the actions you take, which are largely the result of your beliefs**. This is why some of you go for very large goals, while others go for smaller ones. Those of you who actively chase those large goals — often called impossible or unrealistic by others — are ready to undertake the impossible because you have most likely witnessed some amazing things in your past. These observations have led you to believe that you too can make the impact you envision and wish for.

The people who want to innovate believe that they can do anything they set out to do. For example, someone who wants to start a restaurant does so believing he can make money with this venture, as other individuals in the past have accomplished just that. This sense of belief is something you acquire from your environment. What you have witnessed as possible — what you see those around you accomplish — are observations that translate into belief and information. If you see ghosts in your house, then you believe in them. Even though you cannot prove what you saw, you certainly believe in it and no longer rule it out of the realm of possibilities. Others who have never seen ghosts simply dismiss the information. They don't possess the need or desire to know anything about ghosts. But those of you who believe in what you experienced become ghost experts, because your belief pushes you to seek out more information to validate what you witnessed.

You define success based on what you believe to be possible. This is why hearing of others who started with very little, yet accomplished a lot reinforces your belief of such a possibility. You might think that you are just relating to that person, but the truth is that the energy you feel when you read or see a story about such an achiever is your mind's way of redefining its possibilities. Just like everything else in all three Circles, belief is based on what you witnessed in your environment, which includes those around you. This is why surrounding yourself with successful people helps you become successful as well. It's not because they will give you money or help you achieve, but their constant "can do" attitude and their reach being so large makes you believe that you can also belong to that class and achieve big goals. When you believe, you seek information. When you gain information, you act. All of these observations and information lead you to design a roadmap for success and often makes you aim for bigger goals than you thought were previously unreachable.

As you grow older, your beliefs are more impacted by your friends or entourage. However, in your younger years your family's beliefs exert the most influence. Understanding that your beliefs are based on your observations of life's possibilities enables you to keep your mind open to what is possible. Half of the equation behind how belief is created is believing that your point of view could be wrong; the other half is believing that it's just right. If that holds true, then someone else's belief is the same too. For example, you believe in one religion and someone else believes in another, ultimately creating a disagreement until both parties accept that either both religions are true or false. Since we are not all brought up with one belief, we tend to disagree often; but ultimately those of you who remain aware that belief is subjective to perspective can anticipate others' reactions based on their beliefs and then manipulate your environment.

Since belief originates from the vision of life you have coupled with your understanding of the information you see, then what keeps you from seeking information regarding things you don't see yet? Not believing in one religion doesn't mean you shouldn't make the effort to learn about its history, rules, and customs. The more you know, the more you can relate to others of that background or culture and understand their viewpoint of life. If you understand other people, but they don't understand you, it gives you a unique perspective to leverage or tweak the situations you are in to your liking.

There is a specific example of this I use all the time. Having been in the finance industry and involved in the automotive industry for most of my life, I understand how both operate. What you may or may not know is that dealerships make money off the car, the extra warranties, and the financing. Even though at times they cut you a good deal on the vehicle itself, it is because they know they will profit on the back end. Knowing this information as well as how much the dealer paid for and invested in a car, I can confidently walk into a dealership pretending to be lost and confused. I make an offer very close to what the dealer has in the car and pretend to want to finance the car. So the dealer thinks that despite making a hard deal, he will make money elsewhere. He accepts my offer. I then walk into the after-market department. I have no intention of purchasing any of these products, but I show genuine interest in them and select an additional warranty package where the dealer profits nicely. When I get to the finance office, I play poor and act as though I cannot afford my monthly payments and force the finance manager to lower the car cost itself, and force him to remove the warranty as I clearly cannot afford it. At this point the car itself is very close to the price the dealer paid for the car, giving them very little profit from the transaction. I agree to a higher rate than I typically qualify for so the dealer feels confident in the deal. Prior to finalizing the deal, I take out my checkbook and write a check for the down payment. I tell them that if I can't come up with the rest of the cash, they can start my loan. Of course, I walk in a day later with a check for the balance of the payment. This strategy enables me to not only buy cars at a minimum cost based on their true value, but saves me the hassle and time of attending auctions to get a comparable value. This form of manipulation doesn't impact anyone negatively, but helps control my environment to get the desired outcome.

The point of that story is not to teach you a new car buying strategy, but instead to show you how you can manipulate your environment based on your beliefs and of those around you. If you know how others think and act, then you can tailor your approach to fit them just enough to get what you want. Despite not being exposed to every aspect of society, there is value in obtaining information about things you are not directly involved in. This information expands your viewpoint and your beliefs, which enhances your chances of being in the "known" and having fewer setbacks.

The long-standing American dream is based on the belief that anyone can make it in America. Where did people get that idea? Did they know people in America who made it? It is primarily because from a very early stage in our society, America has been known for welcoming immigrants into the country. Since work wasn't available in their homelands, these people came to America to make a better living. Slowly, immigrant entrepreneurs revolutionized the world, and other immigrants witnessed the lives of those individuals as a result. Seeing other immigrants succeed on the same mission prompted people to believe that it is possible to be the American success story of starting with nothing and making it big.

"That you believe you can or can't, you are most certainly correct!" — **Henry Ford**

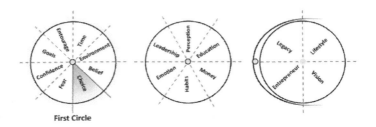

First Circle

Choice

Once you realize that your environment doesn't dictate where and how you end up, you can accept the fact that belief is just information translated into acceptance. Then you are faced with Choice.

Choice is the third element of the First Circle and plays an interesting role in your life. Just about everything you do or don't do in life is a choice you've made or will make. Even not doing anything is a choice.

The first choices you make in life are who you see in the mirror and what you have or don't have. Some of you never move past this stage, because you don't accept your circumstance, also known as your baseline. You sit there and blame the world for your current situation and grow bitter instead of accepting your opportunity for growth. Even if you are not one of them, we all know such individuals. They are usually very negative and often have poor relations with friends and family, whom they blame for their shortcomings. Others, however — no matter how poor, rich, healthy, or intelligent — **accept that regardless of what they do, their past is the past and cannot be changed. More importantly, they accept that their future is in their own hands**.

When you finally choose to accept who you are, you obtain the ability to choose the changes you want to make in your life. These changes can be anything from how you act or react, to things you want or don't want to be part of anymore. You can choose to change your behaviors and actions, let go of addictions, and make more choices that lead to your improved self.

After acceptance, the next set of choices is often based on things that you want rather than the need to improve. It is true that most people can be greedy in this stage, so it is natural for many of their choices to benefit only themselves — such as choosing to be rich and have the luxury lifestyle. Choosing to look past personal gain and vanity and instead making choices towards self-improvement is the way to truly impact your own life if you wish to grow faster.

The choice to be rich is an important one, as it means making the conscious decision to align all your actions to the choice you made and believe in.

You have to make a conscious choice to go from survivor (someone who spends each day hoping the next one gets better, but ends up just continuing a settled life) to a builder (someone who makes each day count more than the previous). You live your life conforming to society such as earning a paycheck, being part of an organization, having a family, etc., but as a result you often become only a survivor. These are the people who live to see the next day as their only choice is to be comfortable; therefore, their goals are often small and can be reached quickly. They don't make significant progress in life with these baby steps.

When you become successful and choose to go from survivor to builder, you accept that your life is in no one's hands but your own. So, you choose to let go of all the fluff. You choose to pursue success and ignore the rules that confine the world around you. You decide that your high goals must be met at any cost, and that distractions in your environment do not dictate who you are or who you become. You certainly choose not to allow your environment to distract you from your goals. Choosing to go from survivor to builder is a choice you must make at some point in your life if you plan to achieve self-actualization, which is realized by those who live, not just exist. When you are more aware of the world you live in, you can make the decision earlier on in life.

Some of you will graduate this circle much faster than others. You do so by focusing your choices on repairing and strengthening your shortcomings, so you can build a stronger foundation for your own future. If you bypass the choice to change and instead accept who you are, you never seek to improve your core or obtain the skill sets you lack based on your past and need to succeed. Many of you move forward to attain your goals before taking a key step: reflecting on what is necessary in order to reach your goals. Instead, you make one attempt after another to achieve rather than slow down and analyze why you made the choice to begin with.

Those of you who focus on establishing the foundation of your life first can put yourself at a huge advantage by choosing your competition from a very early stage, and your competition is yourself. By doing so, you are in the constant pursuit of perfection and reach higher and higher with each attempt. Ultimately, you are better equipped to achieve what others cannot, because you made the conscious choice to grow and live rather than survive and exist.

Making those choices early in your life allows you to align them to your goals in order to keep moving forward — until you hit the roadblock of fear.

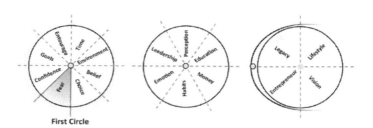

First Circle

Fear

Once you define success, believe in the possibility, and make the choice to succeed, the environment you live in is no longer an obstacle. Then comes the single greatest emotion that you must learn to control and conquer — fear!

What is fear? I consider fear to be the strongest emotion, because it often contributes to all of your other feelings. Fear is often mixed in, and at times hard to separate. Fear exists on both a conscious and subconscious platform and is present in all aspects of your life. From a very young age, you observe fear all around you. There is almost no one who overcomes all their fears in their lifetime, yet many learn to look past and confront them. As a child, you witness this phenomenon and the emotional rollercoaster through your parents, friends, and relationships.

Think about the fear that a child goes through when separated from his parents before going to school. As the child gets older, he finds ways to manage fear by making excuses like having stomach pain in order to avoid going to classes he didn't enjoy. This might have even carried on into high school and college years with different reasons attached to it. In the context of relationships, you might have witnessed your parents fighting, separating, or divorcing; therefore, you developed a fear of marriage. You choose to stay away from that commitment based on this fear that it will simply fail in the same way you witnessed your parents' relationship fail. Fear of failure can be attributed to why you do not start your own businesses; you are afraid of all the work you put in without guarantees. The lack of self-confidence is once again related to fear and all of the poor decisions that come with it.

Why does fear play such a large role in your life? Fear acts like paralysis to your mind. The more you think about it, the more you freeze. You can't act in any context, and so you fail. Since everything in the world involves making decisions, fear consumes a large portion of your life. When you over-analyze things out of fear of making the wrong choice, you give yourself many reasons to take no action. If you think about your earlier years and how many times you passed on opportunities or didn't act out of fear, you will notice that all of your dreams could have come true by now if you had taken action instead of succumbing to fear of loss.

A good place to see this fear represented is through people's spouses, relationships, or significant others. How many times have you wondered how a good-looking person is with an unattractive partner? You probably have your own theory of why that is happening. Now, I certainly understand that beauty is not only skin deep and also in the eye of the beholder. Nonetheless, there is a general notion of what is considered beautiful. If we think about those individuals who settled for a life that certainly wasn't what they had originally envisioned, then we can understand the reason they did so was rooted in fear. The same can be said of those of you who fall in love very easily. Fear of being alone drives the emotion of love to manifest itself faster. If this fear is powerful enough, you settle for what you have or what is accessible rather than seek exactly what you want. When you become that Settler, you find yourself unhappy with your choice in the long run. You realize it was driven by fear and not the right fit.

The interesting part; however, is why you let go of this fear after the fact rather than before. It is primarily because at some point you are reminded of your potential when you meet someone more to your liking or your actual desire, and in return that person shows interest in you. Awareness kicks in that better options were available to begin with, creating the courage to seek what you want rather than what you had simply accepted.

Fear is observed heavily in your early teen years through your interactions with others. You fear failure in classes or activities you are not very good at. You fear rejection and don't ask attractive or popular people on a date. The types of fear we observe are divided into those two types.

1) Fear of Rejection

Fear of rejection shows when your parents are declined for benefits, the job they wanted, or a mortgage. You see people being rejected from athletic groups, certain circles of friends, someone rejected and perhaps ridiculed after asking another person on a date; so as a result, you don't graduate past this fear. Your confidence in your abilities never expands beyond the limits of your fears.

As explained earlier, the reason those individuals settled for what was in front of them was because they never moved past this fear. Their past rejections made them believe they were only as capable as their past accomplishments, which in this case would be very little. If you also think about peer pressure when it comes to alcohol or drugs, fear of rejection becomes a much larger problem as public acceptance is very important to the people who suffer from this fear. Gang members prey on individuals who have not overcome fear of rejection. They provide a welcome inclusion for people who have been rejected, especially at a younger age. Everyone wants to belong, and no one wants to be alone. Every opportunity to belong is one that those with more fears accept without applying logic.

When you overcome this fear, you become more selective as to what you want to belong to, because you believe more opportunities will come. You recognize that choice is an option, and you simply don't settle for anything.

2) Fear of Failure

Fear of failure is linked to fear of rejection and is observed throughout childhood. Failure is observed all around you and misinterpreted by society. Failure in business, failure in marriage, and failure in education are looked down upon. Many parents don't adequately address failure with their children. These youngsters don't understand that greatness isn't achieved in one try. People who don't leave toxic relationships are usually in that situation because they initially feared rejection. Letting go of a bad relationship would mean admitting failure as well as starting all over again. So they stay; ever the Settler.

Entrepreneurship is similar in that many would-be innovators have ideas they want to undertake, but very few succeed or even start. The unlikelihood of success and the lack of guarantee that all your hard work will pay off prevents them from pushing ahead. This fear of failure is the reason some people remain passengers in life; they react rather than steer their lives forward. If your past environment included individuals you observed taking many risks, then you are more likely to take leaps of faith. I witnessed my mother move from country to country without any fears or regrets. She didn't have much money and assumed significant risks each time. I also saw her start multiple businesses without having the necessary experience. While these may not be the best ways to go about living, they certainly contributed to why I can assume much more risk than others and can boldly approach my life. Others watched their parents complaining daily as they follow the same 9-to-5 routines. Or they have observed individuals who don't take risks, and as a result they don't feel that taking risks is needed in order to progress.

If you relate fear in general to being born into a wealthier or less fortunate background, then you can identify different fears that consume each group. When you are born with less money, the fear of failing your families and not making money is supplanted by a boldness that pushes you to take significant risks. You feel as though you have no choice but to stare down that fear.

On the other end, being born into wealth increases this fear. The children that are "privileged" fear that they will jeopardize all that was previously built, and so they take a more conservative, low-risk approach. These fears follow you as you grow older and continue to haunt you in different contexts. You can actually predict the path of one's life once you understand this concept. Look, for example, at the stereotypical assumption that African Americans from rough neighborhoods will become criminals. Race holds no weight. How you were brought up — not the color of your skin — contributes to your life choices.

Risk is a necessary part of your growth, and fear is the sole reason you don't take risks. Awareness of these two realities will help you understand why you are holding yourself back from exploring more areas in your life. Think about how much more you could accomplish if you weren't afraid to fail. The fear of the unknown is what you fear the most. Not knowing if someone will say "yes" keeps you from asking a person on a date. Not knowing if you will succeed in your business prevents you from starting it. You can counter the fear of the unknown by obtaining information on a topic, which will then build your confidence — the next stage in the First Circle.

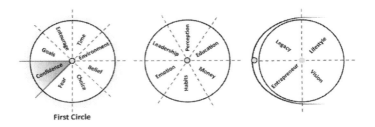

First Circle

Confidence

The unknown drives your fears. It also hurts your confidence. As you can see, all of the categories in the First Circle are connected to one another in more ways than one. Your confidence is a direct reflection of belief in yourself. This belief is based on your ability to overcome fear of failure and rejection, and your ability to understand that the more information you have, the more likely you are to gain confidence and eliminate fear. Fear of the unknown — the most common form of fear — can easily be avoided and overcome with information. As you get older, you receive more information and gain more experiences. All of this knowledge is also how you graduate the circles of life. As you study the Third Circle Theory, you become more aware of the situation and therefore remain conscious of why you do what you do and are the way you are. As a result, you can make the changes because you are aware, fearless, and confident.

Let's say you are a mechanic and notice a rash on your arm that you have never seen before. It looks odd, and you panic that it might be serious. Because you don't know what this rash is, you are consumed by fear that pushes you to seek medical attention immediately. The doctor then informs you that the rash is not deadly; a simple cream will cure it. The rash is still on your arm, but its cause and prognosis are no longer unknown. The panic leaves your body and mind. You can move on, no longer worrying. If the same rash were to occur on the other arm, you know what it is. The unknown is now known. With that knowledge comes the confidence that everything will be OK.

Now reverse this role. You're the doctor and experience a similar rash but you know what it is; and therefore, have no fear. However, now your BMW breaks down. The fear of the unknown sets in, and the lack of knowledge of auto mechanics shakes your confidence.

The fear of public speaking is very common, but some people manage to overcome it quickly while others never do. Some are extremely confident and don't mind getting on stage, even without first rehearsing. Others won't even step up there. This fear is based once more on not having the information about what happens on stage and being informed enough about the topic for your presentation. If you have never been on stage before or don't commonly practice this skill, this unfamiliar territory is understandably scary. You fear the reaction of the audience. The unknown once more creates fear; fear that creates doubt, which creates paralysis and prevents you from taking action.

Another great example would be to think of your current role at work. If you are in sales or in a product-based environment, then you understand that product knowledge makes you more effective in your role. That is partly because your knowledge empowers your confidence, which is elevated during conversations with clients. The confidence in turn creates more customer buy-in for the product or brand. Product knowledge is no different than self-knowledge. The more you know or believe in yourself, the better you can sell yourself. If you believe that you are great-looking and a great value to anyone's life, you see no limitations as to whom you seek for a partner. You believe you deserve someone of similar values as yourself. This confidence is demonstrated in your approach to others and quickly translated into energy that is extremely attractive to others.

This is why some not-so-average guys end up with supermodel girlfriends, or vice versa. One partner showcases high levels of confidence that the other person lacks. The person with the most confidence knows exactly what they want and why they want it. While it may not be a match of similar value, the other partner's lack of belief in themselves makes them wonder why someone would find so much interest in them. So the less confident individual seeks information about that person and sees past the initial physical perception. They believe that value equal to their beauty exists elsewhere with this individual who approached them.

How do we build confidence to progress to the next phase? Confidence ultimately comes from experience, exposure, and your ability to look beyond your fears of the unknown. To gain confidence requires practice. Your ability to move past your fear of rejection enables your mind to practice the act by doing all the things you are uncomfortable doing, such as interacting with others or speaking on stage. The more you practice, the less fearful and the more confident you become that being successful is in your hands. With time and practice, you will do better and better.

Practice turns the act into routine. Similar to the mechanic with the rash, you make the outcome known, which builds the confidence to handle the situation without fear. Your self-confidence can be increased with the constant routines of strong work ethic, productivity in your day-to- day life, and unwavering awareness of your well-being. It is also important to increase the amount of self-education. The more self-confidence you have and the higher the goals you set for yourself, then the farther your reach extends. Once you attain a level where you think you can undertake anything, you spark a powerful desire to innovate. Although being in the First Circle means you are still a long way from accomplishment and fulfillment, you start building a foundation for the traits needed to succeed in the long run, helping you get closer to the life you seek.

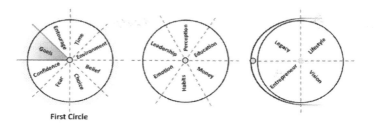

First Circle

Goals

When confidence is mastered and the fear of failure is overcome, you reach the first phase of finding yourself and defining your purpose. Goal setting is the way to succeed in this stage. You set up small goals when you're young and follow with larger goals when you have the capacity to take on more and larger projects based on experience and knowledge. Goals are not only based on what you see as possible, but also on what your experiences are in the past and what you see as a fit for you and your personality. At this stage of your life; however, you are still in the First Circle. Here, the goals you set for yourself are frequently money-driven or primarily focused on self-gains. Nonetheless, being able to fulfill your own needs at this point is very important, as you simply cannot help others if you haven't been able to help yourself.

Whether monetary in nature or simply practice for a greater gain later, coming up with a list of attainable goals is good practice to guide you toward achieving the greater prize down the road. If you learn from an early age why setting and reaching goals is important, you will go farther in life. The more goals you set and reach, the more your confidence level rises and the lower your fear of failure sinks. This frees your mind to focus on harder projects in the long run and allows you to raise the stakes of what you deem possible — pushing farther and harder every time.

How are we taught to set goals? Early on, you may have been told not to reach for the stars, but instead aim for what is possible. This absurdly limited approach to life may have been passed down to today's newest generations, but it's time to stash it away. Think the possible and you certainly will attain it with hard work, because that is the way the "worker" thinks.

Here is a great example of how this approach is used by Generation X. In the late 1990's, my uncle, a very brave worker and chef, decided to open a restaurant. His sole focus was to bring a successful Mediterranean restaurant to a specific city in Virginia that lacked diversity. His main goal was to create such a restaurant, cook away in the kitchen, and increase profits. He depended on that restaurant for his income, so he needed to achieve the latter of his goals. He succeeded for quite a while, but years later his profits slowed down a bit. Running the restaurant became lots of work for very little money. Eventually, his venture became no different than working for someone else, except with ten times more headaches.

Here is where my uncle failed: his Generation X mindset taught him to create and think for today. Doing so required him to be a chef making great food to bring in more people, which would increase profits. However, tomorrow has brought the need to expand the brand across multiple footprints and platforms while a concept is hot. You can't stand still and expect to compete in today's dynamic culture. Eventually, the entrepreneur just lets go and moves on to a new business while the existing franchise continues to feed money into his pocket.

The ownership of a retail business requires establishing value for a market today and then creating value for someone else tomorrow. You need to build residual income rather than work for money income. A person can only do the same thing for so long without having any changes in motivation or increased profits. While restaurants are great, they are limited to what they produce in income—no matter the type of food they sell. My uncle never understood what his real long-term business plan was. Instead, he knew how to set his goals on having a proper restaurant as he had seen in his past. My uncle never lived in or saw an environment of franchising a restaurant. His mentality told him to create work and earn money, not long-term wealth. He was able to attain the simple goals he set, but couldn't sustain himself over the long run; because, like everyone else, he has limits to what he can do. His vision and practices for building a business is what he experienced and what he will pass on to others who observed him, such as family and friends.

The real difference between Generations X and Y when it comes to business is access to information and clients across a global platform rather than a local one. Even though this new global access exists and is in full effect, very few people set their goals to reflect their potential or set their ideas to take advantage of that. But if you do, you will see significant results similar to how Facebook, Google, and LinkedIn grew so quickly. They all used global resources to expand their brands and targeted the entire world as their marketplace. Innovation is now easier than ever to bring to life as resources, labor, and client bases are worldwide. If your past experiences, learning, and observations have always been of a conservative business, then (like my uncle) you create a business for work. Even though you know it's possible, your mind tells you that creating a product that will innovate the world is not in your destiny to create. What this little voice is really saying is that you're not confident enough to take on such a responsibility.

Think about goals in a global sense, similar to the world's new business model that allows for bigger, better, and further goals than before —loftier goals that benefit more than just ourselves and are set to one day innovate for the benefit or facilitation of the world. As such a goal is fairly large, you need to set milestones to help you identify when you are on the right path to be able to reach your goal. You are in this place where you envision large goals, but at this stage in the circle you do not yet have capacity to take it on. Still, you don't want to achieve anything less than your dreams. Being able to undertake your lifelong dreams and purpose is more than just being able to envision your victory. You must not only understand what the outcome of your project looks like, but also be able to see the road you must travel and why YOU are the one who is best positioned to take this on.

My background was not in education, nor was it in helping people; but throughout my finance career I was able to identify my strength of being able to read and coach people to help grow their talents. As a result, I acquired the knowledge to lead them and established my credentials as a money expert, which allowed me to validate my position in helping them reach a better financial stage. All of these experiences, coupled with a proven track record, increased my confidence enough to attempt to help an entire generation, instead of just 20 or so people a year. I didn't just wake up one day and decide that I wanted to help people without ever having helped anyone. My ambitions and long-term goals resulted from my experiences. My ability to expand past those experiences and align everything together made me that person.

Your goals are a projection of your beliefs, which we discussed earlier. They are highly impacted by your choices and ability to overcome fear, giving you more confidence that you indeed made the right choice — enabling you to carry on until the project is complete and the goal met. Those of you who realize this have mastered this phase of the First Circle.

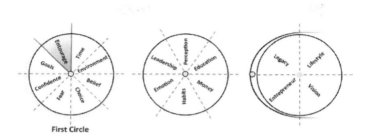

First Circle

Entourage

As you set these high goals for yourself and are driven to succeed, you start to realize that the people currently around you are just not enough to help you succeed. The diversity of viewpoints and their skillsets are not enough, so you seek new friends and individuals for your entourage. Partly because people evolve in different stages, this naturally occurs with time and changes in your life. As you have a major change like marriage, you tend to start making new friends that fit both you and your partner's interests. You gravitate toward other couples, and you naturally attract people who believe in what you believe and who share similarities with you such as status, interests, work, children, or anything else you feel differentiates you from others. In other words, if you see others who share your uniqueness, then you are naturally attracted to them and decide to share your common beliefs, which creates new relationships.

This is how you choose your friends. As you grow, your interests are lifestyle-oriented, but as you grow older you become more serious about life and notice that your interests shift to success, entrepreneurship, and of course money starts becoming more dominant than before. If you show these interests to your existing network or entourage and discover that their interests have not evolved, this creates a separation between you. They might feel abandoned, as though you somehow feel that you are superior to your friends. This is where the line "if you are not going to be around during my struggles, then you won't be there during my successes" comes from. You feel as alone and abandoned as they do, but no matter how you try to reconnect, you simply can't.

Your confidence, beliefs, and goals are now entirely different from those of the people you called your friends. This phase is the beginning of your self-discovery. It is also the time when you are most vulnerable. This is where the self-help industry thrives; it becomes that guidance, friendship, and value you've been missing. It is very easy for you to look up to the wrong people. With the self-help gurus, you want to believe you have found your messiah, your new best friend, and the one who will guide you along the path that is blurry to you (but seems clear to them).

You discover that you want opportunities. Therefore, this critical part of your journey in life can become very sour before it gets sweet. Your desire to belong becomes stronger than ever before, and you seek answers. People like self-help gurus and multi-level marketing companies understand this scenario and capitalize on it. In too many instances, they end up doing nothing more than taking money and time away from you.

This burning desire to succeed coupled with new fears of the unknown, which you haven't ventured into yet, creates this hunger for immediate answers and solutions. Unfortunately, they don't exist. If your foundation isn't strong enough, it becomes difficult to separate yourself from the act of instant gratification. You don't understand and have not witnessed the right behaviors in your past, so you don't have enough information to form conclusions. All you believe in is questioned, and you rarely have the right people around you. As a result, you really don't know whom to trust or rely on.

The need for instant gratification is a like a bad fear — the fear to fail coupled with the fear to be left behind. The fear of failing prevents you from acting for the long term, yet your constant pursuit of catching up to those new people around you makes it impossible to find balance. So you attempt new projects, ventures, and businesses; but never see them succeed. In exchange, you accept the next thing you believe will make you money. This bad habit is one many never grow past, primarily because of their continued fears and their inability to move forward that keeps them in this phase.

Your entourage presents the solution for leveraging yourself out of your fears. Your new observations are similar to the past ones, but take longer. You no longer just accept what you see, but instead question it. Those whom you identify with will make the true difference in your life, but remember that you are hungry for observations and learning. You must be very careful in identifying with the right individuals who can indeed show you the right path, rather than one who benefits only themselves. Select individuals with similar interests, but whose behaviors and success are actually defined as what you want yours to look like. I am referring to people who are doers, not talkers. Those individuals who live the life you want and possess the same attitude toward life that you have must be included in your entourage.

Attitude is important, because belief is more than just interest; it is based on a common feeling towards that interest. Many guys love cars, but not all of them like the same types of cars. That is why car clubs often include similar genres of cars and not all cars. Different people, no matter how common their interests, feel different about those interests. So many different attitudes can be had towards the same interest that it is very important to seek an entourage in business and success with a similar attitude as your own, which we often forget to identify with. If we refer to a young entrepreneur who did well for himself but holds a significant arrogance towards others and runs by himself rather than helping those around him, then it is most likely true that he will always choose himself. His attitude towards success is indeed different than yours. As much as his mentorship will hold some good components, it may also do more damage than you can foresee upfront.

Selecting the right entourage will help you graduate much faster than others and buy time for yourself as guidance and behaviors can be observed faster. Keep in mind that despite losing time, it is better to not go the wrong way only to have to pull a U-turn when you realize you have been misled. Those who maintain the right entourage open their eyes to the Second Circle by observing how others who have graduated the First Circle behave. It looks very appealing, as the next circle is a new world and a new path. Ultimately, it is the strong emotion of greed and wanting to belong to an elite group, which you now have identified and witnessed.

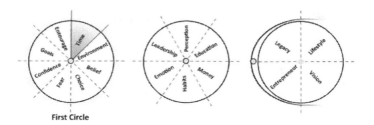

First Circle

Time

Time is the final phase of the First Circle. How you perceive its value is what enables you to graduate this Circle and move on to the next phase of your life. Time itself is something that you often take for granted without even realizing it. While you wait and entertain yourself, others are taking full advantage of their time to progress in society and move their ideas, lives, and beliefs forward.

You might not understand or care about the effect that losing time has on your life. Even if you seem to understand early on that there is no making up for lost time, you don't seem to show an urgency in using your time — unlike the way you feel about money, which from an early age is always the driver of why you do what you do. You go out of your way to attain money, but it seems like you never look at how much time you are giving up in exchange and what that value really is worth.

You may be taught from an early age that you shouldn't waste precious time, but you are seldom reminded of this advice. You are also told that you only live once and should therefore live it up, yet you are rarely reminded of what that means in context. You are also told that living for today and not tomorrow will give you more pleasure out of life, but you're never shown that amazing people still needed ten years to build empires and that each day consisted of building upon the foundation of the previous day. Our foundation and understanding of time is actually not built as much from our observation like everything else, but rather our circumstance and value of money. How you value money dictates how much you understand time, which is where the phrase "Time=Money" comes from. However, how you value money does come from observations and experiences growing up, so it delivers a large impact on your understanding of what to do with your time and the weight it holds on how you make money. Let me try to break down the complexity of time into real life examples.

Let's say Chris was born into a moderate to poor household. His parents have constantly reminded him of how important it is to make money, so he has developed a sense of urgency about it. Since Chris has never been taught the true value of time, he will make as much money as he can in the moment, rather than strategically grow his skillset. So he creates short-term income instead of a longer and larger gain later. His time has no value other than how much money he can trade it for. He also has never had examples or experiences in his life that showed other ways of valuing time. Now, if Chris' entourage had been selected properly, they would have shown him a new way of thinking. The odds aren't great though, because we attract those who showcase what we believe, and the people Chris most likely looks up to are all rich for the moment. Unless he changes his viewpoint on how time can be leveraged for things other than money, he will never learn how to grow instead of survive.

Rob, on the other hand, was born into a well-educated and financially secure family. He has no sense of urgency for making money, but does understand the long-term value of building a foundation with education, time, and money. Partly because Rob isn't dependent on earning money, his understanding of the value of time increases. That doesn't mean he understands what to do with time. Rob knows why time doesn't translate into immediate money and that investing time in other aspects makes sense. This lack of urgency comes from seeing that the family conversations aren't centered on the need for money, but focuses on living well. This perspective can also have a negative impact, because Rob feels like time can be wasted since the lack of urgency means that tasks can wait, so he procrastinates.

Both situations have their positive and negative impacts, like the individual's ability to value time. In either scenario, the individual must self-reflect with honesty as to how they spend their time in order to change and graduate to the next cycles of their lives.

How many times do you hear people around you say, "I just don't have time?" Having time is a choice that is no different from spending money. Similar to other resources that become scarce, time runs out and so does money. You must choose how to invest your time and understand the return you will get from that investment.

If you choose to go to the beach for a whole day, you forego working and making money for the day. You also give up the opportunity to further educate yourself on something new, develop an idea or business, network with others, or any result-producing activity you could have done with your time. You have to ask yourself if the beach day was worth the exchange. How did that allotment of your time align with your long-term goals?

Here is a clear example of how you have to think about the value of time:

You own a company and lack the manpower, money, and resources to build it up, much like every other great start-up in the world. Spending an entire day at the beach removes you from the business and prevents you from moving forward on the foundation you are building. Now, if you feel overworked and unproductive, relaxing on the beach to recharge your batteries is a great use of your time.

The same decision to go to the beach can be viewed in two different ways — one is productive, while the other is lazy and selfish, but both end with you on the beach. Based on your self-awareness, you must find balance so you don't create false pretexts and actually end up on the beach daily without making progress.

Choosing how you spend your time enables you to gain more information, helping you accomplish more in a day than most people. Imagine if you go to work and actually work 100 percent of the time — which is highly unrealistic, but think about how much more you would get done. Imagine how many more bonuses, promotions, and information you could gain.

Now imagine you worked only 60 percent of the time you are there, as many productive Americans do. What is happening to the other 40 percent of your time? It is being thrown away? No positive outcome can come from doing nothing. Since you are obligated to spend a certain amount of time at work, how you use your time matters heavily. You need to learn to be more productive while you're at work so that once you are done for the day, your mind can leave work behind becoming carefree and able to fully focus on other things. You naturally waste a significant amount of time between activities, such as between the time you get home, eat, or perhaps sleeping in until 11AM the next day because you went out until 3AM. All of these in-between times you spend on entertainment and leisure can be converted to productive and effective work time directly aligned to your goals. If you don't go out until 3AM, then you can work until 2AM and wake up at 9AM instead of 11AM and work again for two hours. These four hours alone could be translated into moving your life forward if you focus on what you need and not what you want. The real problem here is that when you are working for the sake of just doing work, you are not yet passionate. You won't find something that moves you so profoundly that you believe its value to be above your own. Once you reach this point, you make the time for it. Think about the last time you were in love. Even though it seemed at first you never had enough time for each other, you somehow managed to be together because you rearranged your schedule to make it work. This feeling of putting love before yourself is what drives you to find more value in creating time or diverting time resources to it.

Most failures in businesses stem from the inability to create resources and put them to good use, with time being the most precious one. When you learn to control how you understand and value time, then you can be resourceful instead. When using excuses like " I don't have time," you're simply rationalizing a bad choice of how you invest your precious time. That choice is based on the other stages in the First Circle — your entourage, confidence, fears, values, and beliefs. All of those together create what you understand to be your value, which you can then divide into the allotments.

We've covered the scope of what enables someone to graduate the First Circle, although very few people do. Unfortunately, the majority of the population stays in this scope of thinking their entire life. They are marked as followers by those of you who do graduate the first step of your life. If you think about the word "follower," you envision someone who does not take initiative, someone who follows the norm or the path that others have provided them to travel. Think about the three titles I told you about earlier: The Birth, The Settler, and The Dreamer. All three have follower-like attributes; none of them reflect a person who shows initiative. When you are born, you are born by someone else's action. However from your youth, you can choose where you go in life. Perhaps you feel it's easier to settle and follow others. When you can set goals, you fear failure and choose to dream instead of taking action. You choose to not take ownership of your outcomes and move through the three stages of the First Circle rather than graduate to the next. The lack of action is also a choice that keeps you in a life dictated by the vision of others.

The real difference between goal setting and dreaming is very similar to the difference between those in the First and the Second Circles. It is the power of actions and reactions that come from them. Many could argue that setting high goals for yourself is the same as dreaming — and they would be wrong! There is a similar possibility that your goal is the same as someone else's dream. Many people dream of owning a million-dollar home and others set goals for the same, but the two individuals and the two actions cannot co-exist. When you dream about an accomplishment rather than aspire to work towards it, it is because of your lack of confidence in yourself and your inability to reach it. Therefore, you simply envision a dream of possibilities. Your vision of yourself and your abilities make you feel like it is unreachable, and thus you take no action towards it. It remains just a dream.

On the other hand, if you graduate the First Circle, you see the dream as a goal instead — something you can see yourself reaching. Long or short in nature, you believe yourself capable of reaching it. You know that your actions will eventually lead you there no matter the time it takes to actually reach them. The main differentiator is that action is what drives results. You are past the stage of dreaming.

The First Circle individuals lack the ability to take ownership of their lives and constantly blame their environment for inaction. You will often hear them complain about being the victim and disliking things like their job or living situation. They place the blame for their shortcomings on others whom they believe don't understand them or recognize their value. These First Circle residents fail to realize what the American dream is, because they don't see that it is their work that will create their new story, not their environment. The idea of change, growing, improving, and progressing in life comes from your ability to understand that you are the driver of those actions. You and you alone incite the reactions that result. Your laziness also has a reaction and can mean that you remain in the First Circle.

When you take ownership of your role and your future by overcoming those eight attributes and being honest about where you stand, then you can make the conscious choice to improve through actions and information. This leads you to see more of life. When you remain in the First Circle, you live in a world created by others and are not capable of seeing their plans for you. You follow the path rather than seek out the shortcuts to beating the odds. Think about the circle itself and my earlier description — the belief that the world revolves around you at all stages in the First Circle. It is because you are both self-centered and selfish. Yet some people thinking that the world revolves around them still don't do anything at all. If you believe that you control the world and yet take no action, then what can possibly happen?

The First Circle Summary: It defines who you are and what type of personality or skillset you possess. It is all about learning, growing, and understanding more about yourself. It's about you and the fact that the world does revolve around you, which in this case is ok and you shouldn't be expected to do any more than just that. Between your entourage, your time, your goals, etc., it is constantly focused on you.

If you are still in the First Circle, you might feel that you are not progressing at your work; your routines at home don't become better with time but instead are prolonged. You struggle to find your voice at times and know you should speak up. You often look back at your choices and wish you could change your past actions. You often find yourself torn between doing the right thing or just the right thing that will benefit you, and in most cases lose that battle with yourself.

The Second Circle

Let's move on to the attributes that a person gains after they graduate into the Second Circle. Keep in mind that there is no set pace to move through the Circle or to graduate from one to the next — or even a guarantee if you will. The only constant is that everyone starts at the First Circle. Most people experience cycles in the same manner and build upon experiences the same way. Some will make quick progress, but the majority won't even understand the existence of the Second Circle until much later in their lives.

Here is an example: some people don't buy their first home until their early 30's while others buy them earlier. The majority buys them around the same age partly because they graduate school at the same time (four years after high school) and have a few years to build an income to become financially responsible enough to buy a house.

This methodology to life's cycles can be identified in more ways than just money. There are systems and matrices in place for government, corporate America, finance, marketing, etc. Just about everything you see is part of a bigger picture that has been created systematically by someone else. These systems all tie in together to create a society, and every person and every institution or organization plays a role in this society (like it or not). More importantly, everyone chooses their role (which is why you choose what degree to earn or job to apply for). From there, you keep playing or change your playing field. The bigger consideration here is that society itself doesn't dramatically change, but its structure and how you function within it does. New fields, jobs, and support groups are created. New innovations enter the market, changing the playing field and rules, but not the market itself. This is what you call "innovation" and "progression," and with each change comes opportunity. To identify opportunity, you must not only understand what these systems are, but also recognize how they function so that ultimately you can gauge where you fit into the mix. In order to do so, you must increase your awareness to your surroundings.

This awareness comes from the six attributes found in the Second Circle: Education, Money, Habits, Emotions, Leadership, and Perception. Good education and money play a significant role in the Second Circle. If you have more access to these two things, you get a slight head start. They hold more weight than some of the others like emotions and habits, which are learned more quickly by those born into families with less access to education or money.

Regardless of any handicap you have from the circumstances you are born into, you still have to master each element in order to graduate to the Third Circle. Since only two percent of the world reaches this pinnacle, don't be too concerned if you still have a ways to go. Most of the planet will continue to live within the two first Circles. Even though this book should help you realize "how" to move past the Second Circle, you certainly have a significant amount of work ahead of you once you get there in order to reach the Third Circle.

The Second Circle focuses on the Awakening, the Leader, and the Achiever. Despite the fact that most people manifest traits of each attribute in the Second Circle during their First Circle cycle, they don't belong to this circle just yet. Before you make the shift to the Second Circle, you must grow your awareness so that you are no longer reactive to society and can hold yourself accountable for those you lead. You also need to understand how to achieve and innovate. Here are the attributes that will enable you to do so.

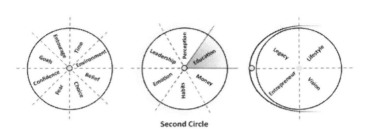

Second Circle

Education

Education is a vast topic because it is almost never ending. When you think of education within the Circles' context, think of information you gained rather than formal school-based programs.

When your mind overcomes the attributes of the First Circle, you can identify those concepts we discussed earlier. By applying your curiosity, you start questioning why things exist and what their purpose is. You attempt to understand which system they belong to.

Curiosity feeds the need for answers. Our minds naturally seek answers to eliminate fear. Refer back to our mechanic/doctor story earlier and put yourself in the doctor's shoes. If you were about to purchase a used car, you would investigate all there is to know about the car — its maintenance, history, and more — just to be better informed about your purchase and to eliminate doubt about your decision. This doubt is another way of saying you're afraid of making the wrong decision or afraid of what may happen as a result. With curiosity and doubt, you need to investigate so that you feel empowered to make the right decision. In reality, all you are doing is removing the unknown element, which we discussed earlier as being the primary creator of fear.

Seeking information is easy, and many sources exist all around us. From the education we receive from friends in the industry to the internet, we seem to be good at finding information, but often need that information repeated in order to validate our belief of what we see, learn, or hear. This is why the education system is progressive in nature. It is designed to enhance and reinforce previous learning with new learning, thus increasing your belief in the information. Your belief, which we discussed earlier, has a significant impact on how you receive information, so even though information may be factual in nature, you will not entertain it if you don't believe it. This is why people in the First Circle can be very narrow-minded in their perspective and don't graduate past the First Circle. It is partly due to the emotional connection to your belief, which prevents you from accepting an alternative point of view. In order to receive and accept information and enable it to help you see more of life's cycles, you must release your emotions towards those beliefs and instead consider all information as true or false. Remember that what is true to you may be false to someone else, and vice versa. Alternate realities exist strictly based on what you see, and we all see differently as you identified in the First Circle.

Education exists in three different segments of your life. There is a grand scheme behind one of them, the one you are all forced to attend during the first 18 years of your lives.

Formal School education teaches us how to live and survive within our society. It is the first exposure you have to tangible simple business information, because at a young page you are told to observe your parents and look up to your teachers as respected individuals. Our philosophies as a society have been to respect and elevate teachers into "know it all" individuals who help your parents educate your children. By receiving information from them, you are supposed to develop a better understanding of society with the ultimate goal of choosing the path to take to make your own contribution to society.

Nonetheless, the paths and roles you can choose from are all part of life's grand designs that were previously created by others. There are pre-determined paths if you wish to take on the unknown or perhaps do not wish to be part of the grand scheme. If you have been labeled an "outcast" because you failed to graduate from school, you have been singled out for your inabilities when in reality you just never had the desire. Somehow you view this lack of a single accomplishment as a failure and allow yourself to feel shame. This is the reason why rags to riches stories tend to be so inspiring to everyone who feels the same about education or has no access to education.

Earlier, we discussed the difference between those born into different monetary circumstances. Your observations regarding education from a young age are aligned to your circumstances as well. One is a sense of urgency as a means to an end because of the lack of money, while the other is a path to reach the long term aspirations of their families to keep building on the wealthy foundation they were born into. Think about how segregated universities are in the same fashion. The cost and the connections a family must have to attain a level of education above the rest creates a divide between the various income levels. If your financial status gives you even less exposure to the other side, you continue your one-sided approach. Maybe you must learn from a less expensive community college where the teachers are less experienced. These students have a higher probability of quitting, because the value isn't there. It doesn't make sense to stay unless a very strong reason keeps them there, as belief alone won't. Your success here ultimately comes from your ability to tolerate your circumstances until you are able to change sides and learn more of what's out there.

As you evolve, you might learn faster than others that education — even if formal or expensive in nature — is nothing more than a compilation of information. If you accept that information to be neither true nor false, then your mind is freer to absorb a lot of information. When you can understand that the information provided is only generic and that more information certainly exists on the topic, you start to crave and seek more, thus advancing your education. This is usually how a college student identifies which major to pursue in college or the field to work in. The reason that professions like police officers, firefighters, astronauts, hip-hop stars, and doctors are more popular among youngsters is because those professions are televised and highlighted more in the media. Curiosity, which is derived from observation, is raised at an early age. Through further education and information, you will come to the realization that those professions might not align to your skill sets. Your lack of confidence prevents you from pursuing your dreams, which at that point are nothing more than dreams since you don't see them as attainable.

As you choose to further enhance your scope of information, you seek a different type of education. Through **self-education**, you discover that information flows quite freely on just about every topic. Unfortunately, it is easy to mix opinions with fact when finding information, and accuracy becomes hard to distinguish. But let's think about opinions and understand what you attempt to distinguish. Isn't all information someone's opinion of his or her own reality?

At some point or another, a formulated opinion became an accepted view by the masses, and then grew into a fact. The beauty of self-education is that it is more about personal opinions rather than proven information. It is one way to look at a certain situation — and only one. If you hear the same information over and over again, then you eventually accept the information and don't seek an alternate answer or more information. However, if you differ with one man's opinion, then you continue to seek more information. Ultimately, your self-education teaches you how the system works, and you don't just accept the system you are shown.

Diversity initiates innovation, as one man's view of the world differs from another. The more you understand how others think, the better positioned you are to create your own opinion using all you observed and heard. The important factor here is that most people agree or disagree with an opinion but rarely look at it as simple information. They fail to understand that education is not about disagreement but absorption of information. It should not be looked at from any emotional angle even if the information defies our existing beliefs to their core. You are the by-products of your observations and so are people with different opinions and environments. As a result, you see an alternate reality based on the education you received so far. Those with more articulated opinions have often done more research or are more involved, but their information is also derived from someone else's opinion. Education = Information, and this equation is important for growing towards the Third Circle.

Selective education, on the other hand, is when you possess natural talent and choose to seek specific information. In other words, you listened to opinions and understand them but are choosing to look into the abstract and uncover more of what others don't see. Selective education is more about theories based on information and the ability to link together concepts as a result. As your mindset evolves and takes interest in a specific topic, it pushes you to seek the unknown around that subject. This interest pushes your need to venture out where others have failed. You discover a gap of information, which leads you to innovate if you possess enough information and confidence to undertake the issue itself.

Selective education is the understanding of concepts rather than things. It is your ability to identify the connectors of life. A great example is understanding how Ford is connected to Microsoft, and then understanding how the automotive industry is connected to the IT industry. You need to know what IT-related services or products can be created to innovate both industries. Your selective ability to understand one industry sparks your curiosity into the other one. You discover a world that others cannot see, because they don't have your perspective. If you have an IT background, you somewhat know what to look for when it comes to technology in cars. You also know what may or may not be possible in this arena, while someone from the automotive industry will not. This is how companies like Google and Microsoft compete for world domination in the technology sector. Innovation across other platforms is easy once you possess the skill set. All you need is the information that you previously ignored from lack of interest. Looking at a problem through a selective lens creates a new type of information, one that only you can see or seek.

Every successful individual will tell you that they have not only educated themselves on the topic at hand, but also understand how it works. As a result, these people can identify a gap in their segment or a connected segment. Most entrepreneurs find business ideas in a field of past experience by looking at it through a new lens. Most of this curiosity is gauged once again through observation and past experiences. Think about how you looked at your first job. How would you describe it? Now, fast-forward four jobs later and imagine how effective you would be at that first job again. You would be better because your new experiences have made you more aware and capable, which is ultimately why education cannot outweigh experience. By identifying the gap between education and experience and then innovating through entrepreneurship, you will be rewarded with a monetary gain that exceeds what you would get from just "working."

You create a path that is no longer unknown to others and empower those people to seek their own self and selective education to expand it even further.

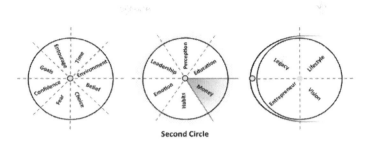

Second Circle

Money

Money is the most constant thing you witness at every age and at every stage of your life, which is why it becomes so hard to let go as you get older. Your entire life at some point or another relates to money somehow. You are told from a young age that you go to school to get a good job to make money, or that you should play sports so someday you can make lots of money. It is frequently the reason you are given for why you should do something — anything. The mere fact that money holds such weight in your entire life reinforces the understanding that making money is perhaps more important than anything else in life. So you value the fibrous paper more than your families and friends at times.

Your focus; however, is not on growing money or even saving it, but *making* it. As an individual, you are "graded" according to your income — classified as high, middle, or low class — and not how you live, which demonstrates how society is consumed by the idea of money.

If you revisit the financial status a person is born into as the baseline for life, you learn from an early age of the importance of money. Whether low, middle, or upper class, your path will include making it as well as include spending it. The only difference is the urgency towards how much of it you need to make. Nonetheless, the message of "making money" is reinforced by all cultures, all countries, all societies, and even by all wealth levels. This is the single observation/message that every person is exposed to.

Money in its literal form is a piece of paper you trade for time. That's correct. You do not trade money for goods. Someone else's time went into making the goods, or preparing the food, designing and implementing a technology, or even writing a book. Outside the cost of goods, you trade this currency for their time as it relates to the item. You pay more for higher quality, because it took more of someone's time or has more value. Ultimately you are purchasing not just the time it took to create something, but all the time it took for them to learn to create something too. If you understand money's relevance to time as we discussed earlier, then you know what your time is worth. Once you understand the underlying truth about money, you start understanding something of more use.

How much are others willing to pay for your time? When you understand that through experiences, you become more aware of how to manipulate your environment as it pertains to money, which ultimately means it pertains to everything. This is the first time your mind grasps perception manipulation. It can often be the deciding factor when you find yourself choosing whether you become a manipulator or helper; it really comes down to your intentions at the end. If you have made money already and not just understood the concept, then you become a helper. On the other hand, when you have yet to apply what you know, you tend to veer towards manipulation as a means to an end. It's a very narrow distinction and often very closely related to the fine line between arrogance and confidence.

Many self-help gurus are born at this stage of their lives. They know how to make money with a great presentation that shows people what they know. What ends up happening is they share with you different ways you can make money, because they know money holds so much weight in your life, making it an irresistible lure. The reality is that they get rich off of it much faster than you; the person actually using the program.

Most people are in the First Circle and don't have enough control over their own lives to understand how to make money. So regardless of how much you teach them about the various methods available to make money, their inability to see things through will make them fail. It won't work no matter how good the system is, but that futility won't keep them from trying over and over again. They never lose the desire to make money, because they are too late when comparing themselves to those who graduated this Circle and feel the need to play catch up.

If these systems were geared towards educated, driven, and professional individuals in the Second Circle, the programs wouldn't make money for the creators themselves. Remember the Settlers and Dreamers in the First Circle and the Leaders and Achievers in the Second Circle; people who can read through you will not be convinced to follow you unless you provide tremendous value. People in the Second Circle don't follow people in the same circle because they won't gain anything as a result. People in the Second Circle follow people in the Third Circle because it is different. Even though different does not mean better, it is an unrecognized alternative to people in the Second Circle. Like everything else, it raises their curiosity and compels them to seek more education.

Like cheese for a mouse, money is what drives you. I am sure you have seen those cartoons that depict food being waved in front of the faces of riding animals to keep them going. Well, the self-help industry and the businesses that teach you how to make money end up doing just that. They wave money in front of you — just enough so you think you can get it. They want you to keep moving forward until you eventually give up. They know your senses and attributes are not trained enough to actually capture the money being dangled as bait, but they do not want you to blame them.

They want you to blame yourself, because you gave up and will most likely try again at some point. The exact same concept applies to the wellness industry and workout fads. The whole point is to show you these systems that take less and less time to get amazing results, yet require so much discipline. Most of the people taking on these systems lack this important trait, which is why the fads work on them.

Money itself is a by-product of how you spend your time and how you create value for those around you. When it's used, it is to buy time; but when it's made, it is to sell your time. If you sell fruits, you feed those around you at a cost; and if you create computers, you provide a tool people use to once again make money so it has value. Based on how well you do, what you create or do might be worth more money to some. You sell your time to an organization when you accept a job. You agree by accepting that your time is worth your pay. You are also indirectly saying that your experience and time as of today has that amount of value. If you sell yourself short, it's because you lack the confidence to accept that you are worth more than what others tell you. **Understanding the value of time and money makes you a danger to those around you and showcases a level of confidence that is unrivaled**.

You are born into the idea that making money is the single most important aspect of life. Therefore, you will focus your entire life chasing it. The problem with chasing money is that you never really understand the value, but instead focus on just acquiring more of it. On the other hand, chasing experiences in life enables you to understand the true value of time rather than money. Those who chase money never find fulfillment, which is why they continue to work just to earn it, even going past the point of having enough to live for a lifetime.

When you follow this path, you become a believer that money is the way to keep score. Why are some people like Donald Trump always on the news? It's because their goal is to define themselves through how much money they have accrued. They publicly keep score, and it helps them.

On the other hand, Sir Richard Branson and Bill Gates rarely make public appearances. They don't prescribe to keeping score by means of monetary gain, but instead through fulfillment of actually helping change people's lives. Donald Trump's publicity stunts put him in the Second Circle; Bill Gates' and Richard Branson's endeavors put them in the Third. They all possess significant wealth. Money as it pertains to the circles is nothing more than leverage. Living in the Second Circle means you know how to make money. **Living in the Third Circle means that money is merely a means to a greater purpose, but never the purpose itself.**

When you learn to make money, you discover what money can help you attain. You certainly understand, like everyone else in the world, that more money helps you attain more goods or comfort. More money is more entertainment, so you become emotional towards acquiring things, particularly if you didn't have all those things growing up. You feel the need to make up for all the times you didn't have toys or designer label clothes, and so you become materialistic and even greedy. This attitude is the direct result of lacking the necessary control over your emotional reaction to making money.

Emotional actions and reactions are the key reasons that people fail or get hurt in general, and the connection is even more so with money. You are so attached to this paper that you value it more than just about anything else. You lose sight of your friends and family when you feel that your money is being threatened. Your inability to detach your emotions from money can greatly harm you. You can see that happen every day all around you. Think about every war in the world where money is the center of attention, divorce where the primary reason is money, and of course crime where the sole reason is to attain money without earning it.

These things do not happen at random. They happen when people choose to make a piece of paper more important than a human life and are selfish enough since they are still in the Second Circle. I want you to understand the importance of letting go of the constant pursuit and emotional connection to money. Instead, look at money as a means to an end rather than the emotional connection of keeping score.

If you look at money in a literal sense and not a glorified one through your past observations; the wealthier you get, the less you actually see the paper money and assume that the numbers you see on a computer screen reflect who you are. This is absurd.

When you see money as nothing more than paper, you then realize that no matter how many times you miss or lose some, you will always have an opportunity to make it. You no longer miss out on opportunities or make bad decisions based on fears of losing money.

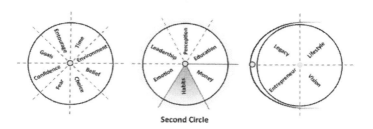

Second Circle

Habits

At this stage of the game, success is primarily defined by how much money you can make in the least amount of time. You start developing habits along the way that will later be very useful to defining your existence. These habits once more are defined heavily by your observations of those in your entourage or those who influenced you. You have now chosen to carefully mimic these new people rather than those from your childhood observations. Observing the habits of the successful folks around you actually helps you more than you think. Their passion usually drives their routines, and they showcase those qualities in almost everything they do even if it's not work related. Habits and talent like consistency, acceptance of failure, balance, and leadership skills are qualities that you must master. At this point in the Second Circle, you can actually see these characteristics in action as if you indirectly had a mentor. The habits you must learn to overcome and make a consistent part of your routine are as follows:

Being **proactive** has a positive impact on your life and has gotten you this far. Think about when you applied for a job or chose to follow through on something you wanted, rather than something you were obligated to do. In order to graduate past this stage, you will have to shift to being proactive. You must decide that hope and faith hold no relevance to your success and actions, but everything that happens is in your control and a matter of acting instead of thinking. Being proactive means more than anticipating; it also means taking action to prevent things to keep you from ending up on the wrong side of the fence. If you think about just about every bad circumstance you have experienced, you can probably easily identify those that you reacted to properly. Can you also look back and understand which of them could have been avoided altogether — requiring no reaction — had you instead taken action to prevent the situation or kept yourself from being in such a position?

A great example of this is the housing crisis in 2008 that struck the U.S. hard. Many people simply let themselves fall behind on their mortgage payments. While that may have seemed like the only option at the time, they could have instead called their lender or lawyer and attempted to find a solution before failing to make their payment, not after. The same example can be applied to going out on a Saturday night. If you know someone whom you've have had confrontations with is going to be at a certain place, stay away regardless of how you feel or how many of your friends will be there. Learn to proactively guide your life to keep you from going places that may compromise your goals. The skill set you must learn to master is the one that allows your proactive nature to think ahead farther than most. Most individuals in the First Circle will think three to six months ahead, those in the Second Circle think one to five years ahead, and most of the people who have reached the Third Circle can see their entire life and how it will play out. The decisions you make are highly associated with how far you can see. It is very true that the farther you can see, the more likely you are to make better overall decisions.

Let's use a good example that many of you can relate to. Think about a job offer you received when you were younger. Back then; it seemed so much easier to decide if the job was the right fit or not. As you got older and received multiple new job offers, you took longer to consider each. It became harder to decide which was best, partly because you had more variables to consider such as family, real estate, and perhaps even where the job would take you in the long run. If you consider many of the earlier decisions you made in life, they were focused on addressing your immediate needs; but as you grow older, you anticipate your future needs and choose differently even if you have to sacrifice your current needs for your future ones. Most of life's experiences have shown you that thinking ahead is important and your value for time has increased too. If you consider being proactive, you anticipate and act and you do so in the best interest of the situation rather than the moment. It is the first moment that you consider others in your equation rather than just yourself, which is a trait of those in the Third Circle. When you think ahead, you take a proactive stance on where you want your life to go, and you start analyzing with every decision to determine if it is going to help you get there even if certain dislikes appear early along the way as a result of your choice.

The final aspect of being proactive is believing everything is in your control. You never allow yourself to be a victim, but instead a recipient of the choices you make. Making a habit of taking ownership of your outcomes is a very important trait that will be necessary before graduating to the Third Circle. The ownership coupled with the extended vision of your life or situation enables you to remain proactive and take a driver's approach to life rather than a passenger's: one you'll need to head straight to the Third Circle in due time.

Being **consistent** is the second habit that you learn to form in the Second Circle. You learn that instant gratification is a weakness, but more importantly, is not allowed in your life. Consistency and hard work lead to positive outcomes, and nothing great is achieved overnight. Being consistent in this case is not defined by doing things like a worker over and over again without purpose, but about how you think of life and your actions. Consistency in your thinking and your goals allows you to make sense of things as you rise to new heights each time. Making sense gives you a good perspective on what you want and what you are doing to get there. Focus will be required to remain disciplined in your approach to success.

Creating consistency for yourself is important and usually comes from observing successful traits of those around you. Similar to just about everything else we discussed, those either in your upbringing or in your entourage through the years influence you to adapt to becoming consistent. In my personal upbringing, I can say that my mother was a great example of someone consistent. I watched her not only work consistently for years, but also stick to being an entrepreneur over and over again despite constant obstacles. Therefore, I am now very consistent in my delivery of actions and entrepreneurial in my thinking. If I look around me, many of the friends or people that I surround myself with are also consistent in their behaviors. So naturally, the behavior I absorbed from a young age is that hard work and consistency are the key to creating the best outcomes. Consistency and the behavior which eventually becomes habit is ultimately your ability to make "not giving up" the actual habit itself.

Confidence and belief from the First Circle play a strong role in your ability to stay consistent and not give up. The more you believe in something and the more confident you are that you can deliver on it, the less likely you are to give up. You have more energy to deliver the same performance consistently, even if it seems to be for a long period of time. When you learn that giving up is not an option, that you control the fear from the First Circle to start building this habit, and you no longer need anyone to cheer you on; congratulations — you found the ticker you need to keep going and suddenly feel a sense of purpose.

It's about focusing on the reason why you work so hard that allows you to retain the same level of drive towards your habits. If you remind yourself often of why you do what you do, you refuel your body and mind to continue forward and remain consistent in everything.

If you find yourself inconsistent, in general you still hold a level of instant gratification from the First Circle within you. You struggle with being quick to change what interests you and change your routines. You never allow something to work, unless it works quickly. One reason is because you never evolved past the fear of not making money. You will continue to make money your priority until you can learn to actually make it, which remains difficult because you're inconsistent.

You can learn to rid yourself of inconsistency based on your belief, confidence, and past success ratio, which is not defined by your business success rate. If you have experienced enough positive wins in your life, then your confidence and belief in yourself almost makes it impossible to give up, and the actions leading to the outcome become more and more consistent with each try. For starters, **you no longer chase money and instead chase victory**, which is a significant improvement in mindset. This is the first sign that true passion is emerging in your life and while not really a slice of any Circle, passion by itself is like an inner body orbiting the Second Circle. It is an invisible force created by the combination of belief, confidence, and lack of fear that launches you toward a new level of productivity.

When thinking of the force described as passion, you must think of the adrenaline of fear — but thrown in reverse. Here is what I mean by that: when you are hanging off a cliff, the fear of death gives you wings and your strength is multiplied by almost five times its normal level. This incredible, never-before-seen power manifests itself to ensure you don't fail. The same reaction occurs with passion, but doesn't require the death part. It simply is the first manifestation of purpose-driven living, which you will later discover in the Third Circle. Failing on your belief is as powerful as letting go of that cliff and is not an option either.

When this force takes over you, it seems like work becomes easy and almost routine, which is why people often say, "Do what you love and you won't work a single day in your life." Love is an emotion evoked by passion; therefore, spending all day doing something you love means you are reinforcing your belief. This never-ending domino effect of love, belief, and passion trigger one another until completion. You can't give up until the end is reached. It is almost robotic in nature and unbelievable to those who have never experienced passion to understand why and how you work so hard. But this power is setting you up for success to the greatest level and allowing an understanding that you have no limitations.

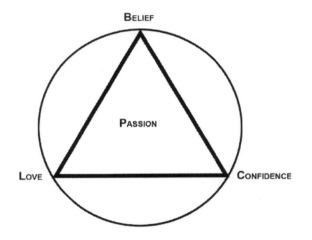

Being Self-Motivated

When you accept that you have everything at stake and cannot give up, the natural realization occurs that no one is going to help you get there, especially since most people live in the First or Second Circle and are egocentric in nature.

They won't help you if it doesn't benefit them, which means you alone are in charge.

You find your ticker as a result, which happens to be your vision of your own success. Then you allow nothing — and I mean **nothing** — to sway you from believing it to be true. This ticker becomes your daily reminder of why you must succeed. It also helps you to remain motivated along the way. In most cases, a person's motivation is highly egocentric here, but that's OK as it is heading towards the Third Circle. Materialistic things will motivate most people until they can look past them. I myself bought a new exotic car each year to remind myself of why I worked so hard. I sometimes put myself financially at stake doing so as I pushed harder to retain the luxury of keeping the car. Even though many might argue it to be a terrible financial decision to buy a new car every year, I believed that purchase to be an investment in myself and not the automobile. This behavior fueled me to keep going, and I can tell you that it certainly helped me despite being difficult. The cars were a symbol to me: a sign of appreciation for where I was going.

You must also find your ticker and what will keep you afloat when you slip down. That trigger cannot be for someone else. Do not make the mistake of working for your children, but instead find what satisfies your soul. While working for the benefit of others is very noble and a big part of the Third Circle, those who undertake this direction early on will burn out and often blame others for their failures. For example, if you work to please your wife only to find out that she is unappreciative, the negative response destroys your self-motivation. The motivating factor needs to be constant and cannot be emotional in nature, or it will be unsustainable. If the underlying influence is out of your control, then it goes against what you have learned so far.

Once you've mastered these habits, you become much more in control of your destination and significantly strengthen your confidence level. You are now entering a whole new segment of your life where control of just about everything you do is in your hands. The phrase "you can do anything you put your mind to" becomes a reality rather than a myth — that is, until you are faced with your greatest challenge: overcoming your emotions.

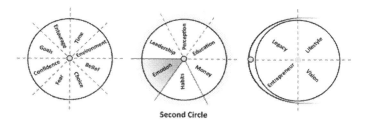

Second Circle

Emotion

"Put your pain in a box. Lock it down. Real men made up of boxes—Chambers of loss and triumph of hurt and hope and love. No one is stronger or more dangerous than a man who can harness his emotions — his past." - **From "An Act of Valor"**

This very true quote makes certain people much more dangerous than others. You hear the line "think with your head, not with your heart" in business quite often, because it is necessary to create a division of your feelings and emotions from your decision making. In life, just like in business, this approach can be used the same way. Imagine how many of your friends or love relationships would be different if you had followed your head and not your heart. Imagine how much time you would have saved if you followed your head, rather than be influenced by your heart. Those who learn to differentiate between the two are able to distinguish themselves from others. This is the center of the Second Circle and the main obstacle you must overcome to proceed past the Second Circle. If you can master your emotions, you will most certainly head to the next phase of your life, one that you will never be able to undo.

Uncontrollable emotions are human weaknesses, but they also differentiate people from one another. It isn't what you do, but rather how you react that makes you who you are. If you think about those of us who stand up and fight

while others sit down and watch from the sidelines; it is the emotions of belief, confidence, and fear that enable some to rise above, while others remain sitting down. The same can be said for just about everything else in life. There are those who fight and those who watch. While everything you learned up to this point is relevant to your ability to control your emotions, it is your awareness that your emotions are your weakness that will enable you to overcome them.

Emotional intelligence is key to taking control of your life and your reactions to life. It is the control of your emotions that makes some people so much stronger than others. It enables you to start transitioning into a world not entirely focused around you. You acquire a taste for understanding others around you and why they are how they are. As you discussed earlier, curiosity takes the better of you and forces you to seek information in order to be at peace, which is how we grow more emotional intelligence.

Emotions are the barrier to your head and significantly change your thinking when allowed. These feelings can keep you from making decisions that benefit the overall aspect of the situation rather than just yourself. If you can never look past yourself, all of your emotions and concerns are centered on you dictating your actions every time. From "I want," "I need," "I like," "I cannot stand," or anything else that starts with "I" reflect a concern for yourself, not others. When you don't like something you express your dislike, so people know you don't want to be in that situation. You do so because you want them to react to your needs and your emotions; you don't really care to express your point of view, but instead seek agreement or an action to make you feel better.

Most of your emotional decisions like people you choose to love or those you choose to work with, even your decisions around money, can be traced back to your egocentric nature that is on display in the first two Circles of your life. Many of you are nodding your heads while reading this section, because one or more of these examples applies to you.

Think about yourself as a child and how relevant it was for you to argue back or start a fight when someone insulted your family member. People were just verbally assaulting you, but you needed to exercise a more severe physical response.

Think about two people bumping into each other in a crowded area like a nightclub or concert. One of them has the absolute need to retaliate against the other if an apology or acknowledgment isn't made immediately.

A significant other dumps you, and your response is to hate that person once you realize you can no longer have him or her. Or that person cheats on you, and in response you cheat back.

You get rejected after asking someone out, and then you no longer feel that person is attractive when in reality, they are still the same person you wished you could have gotten to know 5 minutes prior to your interaction with them.

You receive a bad performance review at work. Your boss tells you that you are doing a poor job, and you get extremely upset once he leaves.

These are all examples of situations that generate a purely emotional reaction. The reason is in part because you are egocentric. In addition, all of those around you have always shown you what being selfish looks like, so you tend to remain focused on your own feelings and opinions. You often process information with regards to how you feel about it. This is the wrong approach if you want to control your emotions and create emotional intelligence.

You can strengthen your emotional intelligence by simply letting go, and what I mean by that is you have to let go past how you feel towards information. You receive information in life by mediums such as news, opinions, commentaries, direct communication, or indirect reporting that you must not have a reaction to. Instead, process it as just information — no matter what.

Having no emotional reaction at all to information is the best way to condition your mind to avoid a poor reaction. When you have no immediate reaction to data, your mind naturally tends to be analytical and consider all the variables. When emotions are involved, the opposite happens and the reaction can't be undone. By slowing down you can more readily accept that people are acting on information, and that they indeed were unable to control their emotional reaction. When they react in this way, they are expecting that reaction to continue. When you learn to stop the continuous flow of emotions, you become a very powerful individual. You understand how to not be vulnerable and why others are weak. As your environment constantly changes and people react to it emotionally, your heightened emotional intelligence allows you to gather all information before creating a reaction. Others however, act on each piece of information enabling them to only combat a small part of the problem, whereas you will actually create the environment you need for yourself to create complete change in your favor.

Your ability to control how emotionally hurt you become makes you a more logical person. You see why people do what they do. By logically interpreting the data, you weigh both the source and the value of the facts rather than how you feel about it. This gives you a better perspective of its meaning. You understand the context of the information rather than what you are expected to do as a result. If you are in a situation where you are afraid because you've been told that you caused something bad to happen at work, fear can set in and panic can prevent action. Conversely, you can understand that someone is just communicating what occurred, not that you are at fault or will get fired. As a result, your mind focuses on the solution rather than the feeling. **Learning to keep your feelings from paralyzing your actions enables you to make better decisions, instead of dwelling on what doesn't work**.

The same example can be applied to financial management and how we think of money — which, despite not being an emotion itself, is the one item we are most emotional about. We love it, become greedy for it, and don't want to part with it. The funniest part is that we allow money to impact our moods more than anything else. When decisions come to mind that are based on money, we respond emotionally as we fear losing it. Think about stocks or investment opportunities; they are missed by many people who can't control their emotions. The fear consumes them, which prevents action. This fear is what you must learn to control and disregard so that it doesn't paralyze your entire life. Otherwise, it prevents you from taking on opportunities around you and from doing what you love. More importantly, such emotions prevent you from moving forward and growing.

Emotional control is so difficult that there are a large number of people who cannot graduate this phase of the Second Circle. As a result, they never truly move on because they're unable to deal with their emotions. They don't get past it, because they believe that the true nature of who you are is how much money you have — or are going to make. They have no understanding of how small they are in such a large world. Those of you who do move forward will understand this a bit differently.

The reality is that as a person, you matter, but only to those around you — the people who know and like you. That in itself also describes how you feel towards others in return. If you like people you remember them, help them, and take time to understand your feelings for them. Take your significant other for example. Those who can't graduate past their emotional intelligence are highly egocentric and selfish.

Therefore, you tend to fall in love and do anything for those you are with. You will fight, pay, and in some cases die for them; but you never understand why. You do these things because of how that person makes you feel. It is for your own benefit, no matter how you look at it. You seek that continued feeling of being loved back. If however, you graduate this circle and control your feelings, then you question your motives. If you would still give your life for that person or spend every dime you have if they weren't your significant other simply because you believed in their cause, then that is a more logical approach than a selfish one. This is also the main reason for divorce; it isn't because of money itself, but how people feel towards behaviors about money (how someone spends money for example) stemming from poor communication around those feelings.

Those who exert little control over their emotions are in relationships because of the benefits or feelings they experience. As a result, they are addicted to that satisfaction. On the other hand, those with more control understand why they feel that way and no longer care about how they feel towards the situation or the satisfaction it brings them. Instead they appreciate the value of the person for who they are, and not for how they make them feel. Therefore, start displaying very strong signs of selflessness in this phase.

Logical choices lead to real results, while emotional choices lead to unstable results. If the example above holds true, then the core of your decision wouldn't change regardless if your feelings had changed (since you made it because of how someone was and not how you felt).

Being able to look past your world, your feelings, your disguise, and your emotions enables you to understand others and what makes them vulnerable. But more importantly, it enables you to realize that you are only as valuable as your actions. If your actions are to pursue money all the time, then your value is not a dime more than how much of it you accumulated.

I see my own value as the experiences I have gone through and my ability to help others. As a result, I feel that I am only defining my existence through how many people I have actually helped. When you think of others and understand them, you will find ways to help them and lead them, which takes you to our next slice for those who move on past their emotions into the core of leadership.

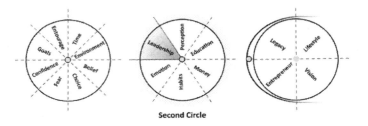

Second Circle

Leadership

When you get to the leadership stage of the Second Circle, it can mean two very different paths going forward — one of the Manipulator or one of the Helper. Even though it's possible to change your mind down the road, you might find it difficult to do so. The choice is usually a result of how you feel towards life and the combination of the experiences you have witnessed to that point. If you grew up around very kind and giving individuals who believed that a good life was about equality, kindness, and helping others, then you will most likely go through serving humanity. On the other hand, if you were thrown in the real world alone and forced to survive, then the exact opposite occurs. Your mind's selfish nature manifests itself, making you more likely to manipulate the world to your advantage — and only to your advantage.

The main difference is not the idea of manipulation, but who benefits from the manipulation. Leadership requires shaping environments, which can be looked at as manipulation in order to function best. Effective leadership benefits the followers first, not the leader. The army is a great example of this, because you have to break down the minds of the soldiers first, and then rebuild them to a stronger state. This strong approach benefits them in combat by making sure they are prepared to face their fears, and in real life because it gives them the confidence and habits needed to be successful.

Becoming a manipulator occurs naturally at this stage of the Second Circle and comes from your ability to control your emotions. This stage takes the concept even further, because you realize that others cannot do the same, which makes them predictable. In this role, you control how others react to certain actions. If you know what makes people laugh or cry, then you have more power over them. This makes you a very powerful and influential person. Influence comes from having what others want or having learned to do what others don't know how to do, which creates an interesting energy based on "belief." You feel that if they've done it, then you can too. For this power to emerge, you as the leader must know what matters to that individual. You must not only show them that you have achieved or attained what matters to them, but also did so from a similar platform. This explains why many of us admire rags to riches success stories. We truly do not appreciate when others who have not earned their wealth brag that they know the way. You simply cannot believe or understand how you can get there; therefore, influence doesn't occur. Then distrust and disbelief kicks in.

This leads us to the next point: great leaders must know how to identify individuals with similar values and beliefs. Without this, the power of influence cannot occur. Influence is a by-product of belief, which can be translated here into mindset. You need to identify with others who believe what you believe and understand why you believe (derived from their values) in order to be able to maximize a group's or following's true potential.

In my corporate career, I positioned myself for success through this skill set. I focused all my energy on hiring people who believed in the same things I did and shared similar values. This enabled me to predict their potential according to the type of personality trait. Based on their backgrounds, I knew who would be most influenced by me, which meant they were more likely to follow instructions and learn faster than the average employee. With this distinction, I was able to win big and earn significant promotions early on. The icing on the cake was that they also advanced much faster as a result. This behavior, although admirable, was one of a person in the Second Circle, as I benefited first.

The same signs you recognize subconsciously when asking someone out or making friends are the same signs you learn to identify in plain sight — knowing who you are or why you do certain things. This differentiates good leaders from those merely claiming to be good leaders. Great leaders know their own signs. They have a clear view of why people should follow them, so their message is precise and rarely changes — only their plans do. Great leaders understand that others don't share the same strengths, tolerance, and emotional intelligence, so they work hard to lead and help them lead themselves eventually.

It's possible for individuals in the First Circle to maintain leadership positions on the job, at home, or in society early on. They might not have yet mastered how to be effective leaders, as they haven't established as much for themselves. Without that achievement, they'll encounter difficulty leading others. While it is possible, it will require the person in that leadership role to have significant strength and motivation. They must also be able to work continuously to improve, which they can do by observing good examples around them. However, these emerging leaders will fail without the support of great mentorship and great leaders. This is why many organizations will not hire young leaders, because there is no substitute for time and experience. This combination allows us to define ourselves as helper or manipulator, and only then can we know our true leadership styles and intentions.

This particular phase we are discussing; however, is not about your role at work or at home, but the skills you develop and your standpoint or view on society as a leader within a system. The system of your life is the one we are discussing here, and even though it's heavily impacted by the functions you hold at work or home, it's not defined by a title or a salary. Instead, this system is marked by how you take charge of your life and hold yourself accountable to those around you. It is very easy to attempt to help others and receive pushback, which can make giving up seem the best choice. But it takes true leadership skills to step back and understand why those following you are having a hard time doing so. It takes the first true act of selflessness to put someone else's life as equally important as your own when they haven't established nearly as much or contributed to society much less than we have. **Being a great leader when all is great is easy, but being a great leader when all else fails takes all the mastered components of the First Circle in order for you to emerge victorious.** This is the real decider that helps you leave the Second Circle and get on your way to the Third Circle.

Imagine how much emotional control and mind power it takes to put yourself second to individuals who, at some point in your life, you believed were well below yourself. Imagine the power it takes to put your own happiness second to others whom you don't even know or have never met. Do you know many — or any — people capable of that?

Here is a real life example of how I exercise different leadership roles every day and define my own life path. In my younger years when I was learning to manage people, I discovered that I had a unique gift for helping people — the ability to shelter my emotions and think with my head. I leveraged whomever I hired, not only to teach them how to be more effective in their jobs, but to also help them be successful in life. As I learned more, I became more effective in my execution. My methods of teaching became less conventional and harsher, but were necessary in order to help others. I put my job on the line every day, going above and beyond my responsibility as a vice president of a company that paid me a handsome salary. I did so because these people were great and deserved great leadership. While many disagreed with me or felt it wasn't my business to help them in other ways, those who did welcome the help will forever prosper from what they've learned. They in turn will help others as well. I chose to take the risk of losing my job for the sake of others learning, and I did that because I developed the mindset of taking action, not just going with the flow. If I wanted them to help me, if I wanted them to be successful, and if I wanted them to be on my team, then I had to make them understand. I certainly couldn't wait for someone else to come rescue me to do what I could have done from the beginning. You as a leader are capable of the same things when it comes to growing talent, but not many will take the risks in seeing the execution all the way through. There are elements like fear, entitlement, and emotions that come into play and prevent other leaders from acting (First Circle people). Their intentions are good, but their ability hasn't grown enough. It would be selfish of me to wait until tomorrow for others to do what I can do today. The risk I take is dangerous to my own well-being but is certainly necessary. My tolerance grows higher with each effort and gives me the strength and belief needed to start something like SecretEntourage.com to help thousands rather than hundreds. It is ultimately practicing what we preach that makes us better, and it is our abilities that are showcased each day that drives the influence we discussed earlier on.

For you to graduate this very important slice of the Second Circle known as leadership, you must be able to put yourself second to those you lead every day. No matter how tough the situation gets, you must still be willing to give up your comforts, pleasures, or well-being for the sake of the bigger picture. This is very important; it's the graduating slice that allows you to move on to the Third Circle, and there is no way around it. You have to take ownership of situations regardless if they involve leading people or simply seeing an action through to its conclusion. The leader in you and your ability to put people or causes ahead of yourself must be understood before successfully venturing into the Third Circle. The next slice — even though is Second Circle-based in nature — is not an absolute necessity in your ability to move on, but an important skill to understand so you can remain steady traveling through the Third Circle.

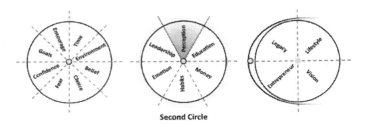

Second Circle

Perception

"Everything we hear is an opinion, not a fact. Everything we see is a perspective, not the truth." — **Marcus Aurelius**

Previously, I explained that manipulation as it pertains to leadership is necessary in order to graduate the Second Circle and get closer to defining your existence. However, there is a component in manipulation that plays a vital role for you in the Second Circle. Although it's not as pronounced as leadership in terms of importance, it is a very important skillset known as the manipulation of perception.

Often used by self-help gurus to bring awareness to their product or service, perception is understanding what other people want, how they think, what they see, and then delivering that to them in a fashion that makes people believe in it. You could think of perception as the tool used to create belief, even in yourself.

As you master the elements of the First and Second Circles, you become a master manipulator of your emotions, reactions, and more importantly of that same environment which you witnessed for all those years. The same environment others witness around you that you are a part of is now no longer authentic, but entirely created as you would want others to see you. Similar to the gurus who use material items such as cars, homes, and watches that are not theirs to create an environment that people desire; they create a false sense of hope for others — in essence, to benefit themselves. The reason this industry is so highly distrusted is the fake aspect of it that some create. In the Second Circle you see that type of manipulation and not only don't believe it, but with your good intentions you see it as people being taken advantage of. You choose to fight it, especially if you have the power to. I myself fight it, because this industry does have a lot of great ideas and content to share, but is polluted by those manipulators who are in it solely for their own self-gain. They ruin the nature of the industry itself.

Mastering perception is critical, even though its relevance to your graduation to the Third Circle is not as heavily weighted as the leadership piece. Nonetheless, it does hold relevance to actually helping you find why you exist. The perception element we discuss is not the same as "fake it till you make it" and has no manipulative trait associated with it. It's more about being fully aware of how others see you, and the message you are selling by just being yourself every day.

So many people are too self-centered to care about how others perceive them, or they act as though they don't. Those who declare, "I don't care what others think," automatically contradict themselves. As humans who haven't mastered the emotional intelligence game, this response by itself is emotional. If you are more advanced in your mindset and have moved through the Circle, you would respond to someone's dislike of you or your actions by asking why. Then you would focus on how you presented yourself to be understood that way. This non-emotional and educational response enables you to tweak your delivery, so you will be closer to the way you seek to be understood.

The Third Circle's definition is about selflessness. Seeing the world without emotional reactions enables you to view the world in its true form unaltered by advertising and politics. Then you must make sure that people understand you the way you wish to be understood. Even though they don't all need to agree with you, you should still be conscious of how others see you. You are moving towards a place where you must examine the world from the outside in, instead of looking around you and moving ahead in the directions you are given. This increased field of vision helps you remain aware to more of what's going on around you.

In the leadership section I explained why people should follow you, and how great leaders positively impact the lives of their followers by keeping their best interests at heart. If you plan to lead others, then you should be very aware of how followers perceive you, so that you understand why they follow you. If you are always portraying the image of money, success, and extravagance, then perhaps they are following you for just that and not from belief in or understanding of what you are working on. Steve Jobs, the co-founder of Apple, made an enormous amount of money and was very influential to those he interacted with, but to this day I couldn't tell you what his home looked like. However, I can tell you that he was a perfectionist and passionate about his role at Apple.

He showed us just what he wanted to be remembered for – his innovations – not the life he lived outside of Apple. His message was consistent with the perception he created. Other established individuals do the exact opposite by showcasing money, cars, and homes. In reality, they often have less than those who don't put their luxurious lifestyles on public display. It is the perception they want others to see of them. This behavior often results from chasing money and if you recall, the ones who chase money validate their existence through how much of it they've made. If you believe perception is based upon money, then you are not ready to graduate from this Circle.

The example of Steve Jobs works well, because he could have chosen to make his life's pursuits about money, but instead he chose something other than himself to portray to others. Ultimately, that is exactly what people remember him for. His legacy will live on forever. Steve truly was Apple, and he represented it even before himself. Almost everyone with an iPhone knows the name Steve Jobs, but how many with Sony computers know the company's CEO? Money chasers are only remembered for money, which means they are rarely remembered at all.

Mastering perception is about understanding the persona you display to others. With time, you learn to control the perception, which makes you an even better leader. Once you are willing to face your flaws and strengths and are willing to see yourself for who you truly are, then you will see the world for what it really is. The people who are not willing to face themselves fear what they might see, but whether you like or hate the circumstances you are in; the faster you accept who you are, the faster you can improve.

The Second Circle Summary: The Awakening, the Leader, and the Achiever are all used to describe the different phases you go through in the Second Circle — and rightfully so. This is the phase in which you wake up from your dream.

You realize and accept your true environment. Your mind becomes aware of the concepts of life. You lead others when you have gathered enough information. For the most part, a strong phase full of achievement motivates you to keep pushing ahead until you forget what you are pushing for. Despite not being good, it is necessary to push forward until you can form a purpose for why you push.

Your ultimate goal in graduating the Second Circle is highly different from the First Circle, where your focus was growth and personal development. While there is room to improve First Circle attributes in the Second Circle, there is a greater emphasis on control over yourself and reinforcement of your logic over your emotions. You must learn to let go of your fears and insecurities and let your emotions remain within your control, instead of dictating your actions or reactions.

If you are ready to graduate the Second Circle, then you understand these concepts and start to understand that **the world you live in is simply too complex and too crowded for it to revolve around just you**. This reality sparks the natural feeling that if your purpose in life is not about just having children and passing the baton to another generation or about making money, then what could it possibly be?

I know that I cannot be the person who tells you what your purpose is, but if you lived in the Second Circle you would know that before you even started reading this book.

What I can do is share with you some unique experiences that might help you understand the path I chose to take in order to discover my own purpose. I can also break down the components that people can identify in their own lives in order to do that for themselves. As I studied the lives and stories of some of today's most well-known business owners, entrepreneurs, and visionaries, and aligned my interpretation of my experiences in the grand scheme of things, I discovered that our paths all shared certain similarities. Those similarities can be acknowledged from experience again, but in four distinct categories that form the Third Circle.

The Third Circle

Comprised of the Vision, the Purpose, and the Rebirth, the Third Circle is all about your quest for the validation of your existence. Despite it not being so clear right from the start, the Third Circle focuses heavily on the search for answers to some of life's most complex questions. When you achieve and understand the dynamics of society, you feel as though you are meant for more than just the same routine of going to work, making money, enjoying life, and retiring. You feel like there has to be more, and that you perhaps need to be the one to break the mold for others.

This is a phase in your life that you can choose to pursue, although you might decide to hold back instead and continue your routine because it's just too demanding to find the answers you seek.

Remember that most of today's greatest inventions — whether technological or process-based — all resulted from someone else's vision, belief, and passion all mixed together to create this powerful energy that enabled them to see it through to the end. Imagine the determination and drive it took Edison to stick to creating the light bulb when he failed 10,000 times. How many people actually have the energy and guts to repeat a process 10,000 times until they get it right?

This powerful force overtakes you when you are purpose-driven rather than money-driven, because while the quest for money eventually gets old, the purpose never does. It becomes a question of efforts-to-reward ratio. If something doesn't make money after a while, then your mind ventures elsewhere and seeks out other options, even if that means giving up that idea or project altogether. Think about Edison.

His goal wasn't to make money, but to create light. Analyze Steve Jobs' mission: it was not to create a computer that would make him money, but to simplify technology. The Wright brothers also had no intentions of building airplanes; they wanted to enable man to take flight. The real difference is that their delivery was not about creating a product to monetize, but to bring an idea to life — in Edison's case, quite literally — and it was often an idea that the majority either couldn't believe or understand. Think about how weird it must be for you to buy into the idea that a man from his garage can take the most advanced technology we have and simplify it, or how about two guys in a barn saying that man should fly. As impossible as it may have seemed back then, these individuals defied the odds and reached for what they believed to be possible, not what society told them they could or couldn't do. They learned not only to live within the dynamics of the Third Circle, but also outside the boundaries of themselves and the Circle itself.

The Third Circle is the final stage of your life's path where not only your existence is validated, but your life is defined by all your past experiences. It's your human side validating that your life was not meaningless. It wasn't for the constant pursuit of money, but for achievement and creating value.

Remember that entering the Third Circle does not mean finding your purpose. Instead, you are working towards mastering the Third Circle itself to define your existence. The Circle contains four essential steps you must take in order to be able to master its concept: Lifestyle, Vision, Entrepreneur, and Legacy.

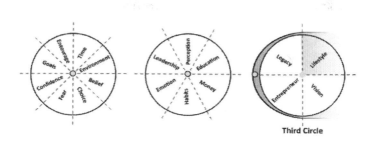

Third Circle

Lifestyle

You've undoubtedly heard of work/life balance and its importance in your growth. **You have a human need to balance what you do with why you do it**, so that you can replenish your energy and continue working harder towards your goals. In my own life, I have always lacked this balance. I am going to tell you why and how I never needed to take a day off. First of all, there is a significant difference between taking time off mentally and physically not going to work. Those who know me will tell you that I travel often, but never take a day off because my mind is constantly on edge, analyzing all I see around me in order to help me find solutions for today or tomorrow as it pertains to my own legacy.

When you reach a certain plateau in life — one where you find enough money to live comfortably — you choose to spend money on things that simply make you happier and encourage you to keep working. These things are not necessarily material-based and can also be based on donating time, investing money, or just about anything else that brings you emotional happiness. About 20 percent of your emotional happiness comes from money. Even though most people pursue money for their entire lives, money itself creates only a small portion of your life's joy. The remaining 80 percent comes from fulfillment. What is odd about this distribution is that despite knowing that money alone does not bring true happiness to people, those with enormous amounts exceeding their needs still choose to seek more, hoping their feelings towards the situation might change. If $10 million didn't bring you happiness, why would $20 million be any different? This is the false hope I described earlier: some wealthy individuals convince themselves that more money will help them determine their purpose, or that making money is what they were meant to do.

As you earn enough money and master different ways to make it, your lifestyle exposes you to yet another very important segment of society. Many people measure success by lifestyle, but that is a highly inaccurate gauge as success looks different to everyone.

There are individuals who spend money on cars, homes, clothing, travel, and jewelry. While that's great, others reinvest the same amount of money elsewhere to attempt to earn more from it. Their tolerance to spending is different based on their past experiences and observations, which forms their mindset today. Consider someone who earns $120,000 annually and another person who has $250,000 saved up but earns no salary. Both can afford to buy luxurious items, yet they each will look at the scenario from different lenses.

Buyer A with the $120,000 income will think of a $100,000 car as a $1,400 monthly payment. Buyer B with the cash reserves will view the car as $100,000 less cash in their account. While they both attain the same lifestyle and items, they each have a distinct reason why they would or wouldn't make that purchase. To the general public, the buyer with the expensive item has money regardless. Technically, the person with the cash is in a much better position than the one with the income, even if they choose to not buy the car. Based on what Buyer B observed in early childhood, he or she may or may not have the tolerance to let go of half of their savings to fund a lifestyle based on luxury rather than necessity. The tolerance to spending will dictate how one person lives and is not a good determining factor of success.

Your exposure level, as it pertains to success, should determine lifestyle. We discussed earlier that experiencing more of life enables you to understand more of its concepts. Lifestyle is the entry point into different worlds that not all individuals are privileged to explore.

If you think about the exposure that people with wealth of over $10 million have — as compared to those with working incomes over $100,000 — you'll see a significant difference. Their global experiences of luxury lifestyle concepts, services, and ideas afford them more exposure than most. As a result, their ideas encompass a broader range than those with a more limited (local or nationwide) scope.

Travel is only one element of how lifestyle comes into the life equation, but it is certainly an important one. This also explains why immigrants work much harder than Americans in this country, as the foreign-born appreciate the value of employment. They worked much harder in their country for less money. Their past work habits to maintain their jobs allows them to excel, while people without that global experience of job shortages have no fear of losing it. They end up working the least possible amount for the comfortable pay they receive, while the immigrants who come here in search of opportunities may choose to continue to work harder instead of taking a step back and furthering their education. The lack of emphasis on educating themselves and pursuing their dreams keeps the majority of immigrants in labor-intensive jobs. Most Americans in good economic times will say that immigrants are needed because no American wants construction, cleaning, farm, or other labor-intensive jobs. Yet in bad economic times, they also complain that immigrants are taking all the jobs and blame them for their unemployment.

This mentality is ingrained in many Americans — blaming others for their misfortune rather than taking charge and accepting accountability. Those who are born and raised in the U.S. and only experience this culture will remain unexposed to the global work habits, economy, and ideas existing all around us.

One more element enables you to leverage lifestyle in your quest for purpose — the daily reminder that you are free (not bound to doing only what you are told, but what you want). You don't buy the house you need, but the house you want; and you let this apply to other aspects of your life. Similar to just giving you an entry point into a new world, the freedom earned with money and through lifestyle enables your mind to wonder and reinforces your understanding of time. You enjoy your time and no longer see the days as burdens and repetitive routines. In the Third Circle you want more experiences, more freedom, and more information, while those who remain in the First Circle only want to wake up to exist through another day.

This key differentiator reinforces all the qualities of the First and Second Circles. Propelled by this distinction, you proceed into the Third Circle with velocity and drive, both of which you will definitely need prior to undertaking the Entrepreneur and Legacy slices to follow.

Here is a quick story about how I leveraged lifestyle in my own life. Over the past 10 years, I have owned more than 35 cars, the majority of which were exotic or luxury cars. While others said that it was a waste of money or I simply couldn't make up my mind, I looked at this experience through an entirely different lens. When I didn't own exotic cars, I always wondered what it was like to be that guy who pulled up in front of the club in a Lamborghini, went on car rallies in a Porsche, or parked his Ferrari far away from everyone at the mall. This curiosity led me to seek ways to become each individual person at some point or another in my life. More importantly, this desire drove me to constantly change cars in order to experience what it was like to own each model, despite the fact that some were superior to others. My choices made no sense to anyone else as to why I would trade up or down. To me, owning these cars was never about finding the right one, but experiencing the feeling of owning them. In the end, I not only learned about individuals who bought each make or model of these cars, but also gained the understanding of how others perceive them — answering the question that motivated me in the first place. It was my way of knowing what it was like to be "that guy" and also motivated and pushed me to unearth new ground in my own life.

Being exposed to lifestyle not only allowed me to better understand people, but also to experience a level of freedom and observe a world previously closed to me regardless of how much money I had saved. I looked at lifestyle as an investment in myself to continue to grow past this unknown world.

Lifestyle opens doors for you so that you can be granted access into new worlds containing new information, which enables you to think globally. You then no longer limit what you deem possible just because you haven't witnessed them. Think about the boundaries of your thinking as wide as the possibilities of your vision.

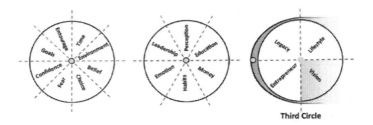

Third Circle

Vision

The Vision shares its name with one of the main three attributes that this circle represents. It will most likely become your obsession for years to come. As mentioned earlier, your ability by now to identify the concepts and systems around you globally is highly advanced. It is now easier for you to see within the scope of five to ten years instead of just one to three. Yet, it is still not clear as to where you fit in the equation.

As you envision what the world could be, not just your current town or state, you seek to take advantage of any missing links. You understand that extraordinary people see more of life, so they should be able to achieve greater things and fix the world's problems since you now see what those are. Now that you see where you fit into the gaps of society, it becomes easier for you to envision what the solutions would look like if patched or fixed. With your new skill set, it is easier to define whether the challenge is a fight you are prepared to tackle.

A vision is a not a dream, but a look through the "what if" lens based on your past experiences. Vision is like your road map to life—or your life goal—and navigating without it will be difficult. If you don't engage in entrepreneurship, it is usually caused by a lack of clear vision. Either you can't see what someone else sees through their vision or you haven't built the skills necessary to have a vision for yourself.

The limited experiences that you defined in the First Circle have left you shortsighted. You can only see one year ahead at the most. Vision is not always based on business ideas and can certainly relate to envisioning the life you want for yourself. But as I said earlier, you must do more than merely say you want a castle and Ferrari one day.

Vision is about believing in the "what if" you can see, combined with the belief described in the First Circle, which comes from enough information to create curiosity and acceptance of the information. If you live in the Third Circle, you are more aware and capable than those in the First. You have mastered the ability to act rather than react and are no longer a by-product of your environment. You no longer sit there waiting for things to happen to you. When you combine your vision with all of the attributes from the First and Second Circles, then you have a strong foundation on which to build your vision. A good path appears in front of you, and the map is clearer than ever. On the other hand, if you see such vision but have yet to learn and master the attributes in the first two Circles, then you probably don't have the skill set required to transform your vision to life. The failure alone in this case will actually enhance your awareness even more and be part of the learning experiences of the First and Second Circles.

Ideas that come from time to time are also not visions and don't act as a driving force strong enough to kick-start the change you seek. Vision only becomes reality when new belief is created — belief which is not already in existence in nature but instead being created through vision. The belief that you will have to get others to follow you using your ability to speak of your vision. Your vision is contagious; it is this greater belief that very few people experience in their lives. As a result, you acquire followers and start an empire. Figures like Steve Jobs, Bill Gates, Henry Ford, Richard

Branson, Elon Musk, Walt Disney, Sam Walton, and many more had visions of what the future could look like if their idea as they imagined it came to life. **Their visions are no different than yours, but their belief in themselves at the time was strong; and their confidence enabled them to launch their empires, despite all odds.** Steve Jobs started Apple from his garage. Walt Disney was fired from his job, because he was told he lacked imagination. Both men became icons that will be remembered forever, because they had the courage to start something they believed in, even though others considered their endeavors a waste of time.

An idea is nothing without a proper execution. Vision gives birth to ideas. Nonetheless, vision itself is an attribute that comes from your ability to see a few years ahead of the 98 percent who live in the First and Second Circles. Because you can position yourself in front of the upcoming change, others cannot anticipate or predict things. Once you do that, you go into my favorite phase: entrepreneurship.

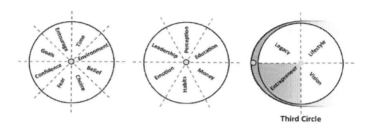

Third Circle

Entrepreneur

The entrepreneur stage in the Third Circle is one of the determining factors for your graduation; all other slices are prerequisites to being able to master this specific skill set. As you see more of life and understand more of the concepts that could trap you, you come to the decision that you simply can't spend the rest of your life building other people's dreams. You feel that you are too valuable from a mindset standpoint to take orders from individuals who don't understand you or your capacity. It is a realization that you want to seek more out of life instead of confining yourself in your comfort zone. There is a growing desire to step away from the mediocre groups in which you spent your younger work years, and you decide to seek the alternative path of entrepreneurship. No job or assignment doled out by others fits you anymore. You realize that you no longer want to be part of the rat race. At this point, you are highly motivated to take on the immense challenge of building something from nothing. Your confidence is at an all time high as you are now navigating through the Third Circle, and the belief in yourself is increasing as you discard all the things you no longer want.

When you undertake entrepreneurship, you do so within the realm of your passion or existing work line. Yet, very often you focus on what you are good at rather than on broadening your horizon. Skills are important, because you can see what you are naturally good at and find ways in multiple industries that you can impact. I spent many years working in banking, leadership, people management, investing, and real estate. When I started making money in real estate and finance, I didn't consider myself an entrepreneur, and I certainly wasn't the type of entrepreneur we are discussing here since no innovation occurred — only income. I only knew how to make money. Despite not working for somebody else, these ventures didn't bring me any additional value over working for someone else. Yes, I was making more money, but that was a selfish aspect that didn't bring value to anyone but myself. While many people consider anyone with their own business an entrepreneur, I have a different view. When I finally focused my energy and skill on leadership and talent management, I found my true passion and what I believe to be my purpose.

Entrepreneurship in the context of the Third Circle is about innovation and advancement, not self-employment. Self-employment is about risk tolerance, not entrepreneurship. Entrepreneurship is about envisioning something that doesn't exist and having the ability and mindset to bring it to life. This innovation must be a new creation and not a bridge to facilitate a technology; those also have very short lifespans and only survive as long as the technology does (which is usually less than five years).

Innovation is the driver of entrepreneurship. It is about giving birth to something new. When you have an idea that you believe underscores the principles of your strengths and changes the playing fields of society, then your reach is as high as your past observations, which translates into belief. Remember that you can achieve anything you believe, but will fall short if you aim low.

Michelangelo said: *"The greatest danger for most of us is not that our aim is too high and we miss it, but that it is too low and we reach it."* You can only go as far as you believe you can go. I explained in the First Circle that belief is based on your past observations, which lead to why you shouldn't take on entrepreneurship too early. So many people want to work for themselves and be the next success story at a young age, but very few people undertake that challenge for the right reasons. They don't have the right mindset, experience, or background; and therefore, either aim too low too early or aim too high without being armed with the ability and past experiences to hit the target. Most of the people who fit this description are motivated by money, not by innovation and value. Winning in entrepreneurship is not about being selfish, but those who focus on money are.

Consider what we discussed earlier about the constant pursuit of money and the reason why this never-ending quest leads nowhere other than just the accumulation of more money. You end up chasing something that will hold no relevance down the road. When you are ready to take on entrepreneurship, it is because you are ready to no longer be a part of the system that society has created for you to fit into. You realize that your mind is so advanced that there has to be a reason for your unique vision. When you embrace that reality, and your vision aligns to your ability, then the most unique gift of them all is born — that gift is called an idea!

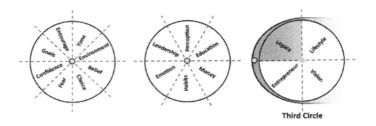

Legacy

The word "legacy" comes to mind when you feel that you've identified your purpose, but legacy itself is very different from purpose. Purpose is based on belief, and legacy is based on education and ability.

Legacy doesn't have to originate from having children, nor does it have to do with religious beliefs or practices. We all want to be remembered, and we somehow feel that children will carry on our name and our legacy. But that logic excludes two critical elements:

- Children will not always carry your name in the way you want to be remembered, and

- It is unfair to expect them to win when you failed by giving up.

When you are stuck in the First Circle and the word "legacy" comes into play, you think of your children or even having children. The reaction is frequently, "I will give my child everything I never had." We want to fill a void in our own lives. I will go as far as saying that it is quite selfish to expect others to accomplish what you couldn't and putting all your dreams and hopes on their shoulders rather than your own.

Understand that your children hold no relevance to your legacy. They will create their own, which will differ from yours, so it will mean nothing to your future.

What you have or don't have does not dictate whether you are remembered or not. What you have or don't have is not a measure of your success or a measure of your intelligence or mindset. It is nothing more than your success rate at mastering the game of society, not the game of life.

It is outlined for you to go from the First Circle to the Second, because society has made it that way for you. They have established all the steps needed to succeed in life and have made it easy for you to know that if you do X and get to Y, then Z is right around the corner. Society has taken the thinking out of being successful; and despite all the steps, roadmaps, and proven strategies there to help us, people still choose to not conform or follow through on being successful. What society doesn't do is make you aware of the Third Circle. This overarching cultural guard actually does a great job of protecting you from seeing it or venturing in the direction of this Circle, because doing so would mean losing you as a member of this system they created. It does so by creating a comfort zone for you through debt and a stable income, and then reminding you of your dependency on this

system to retain this newly gained comfort zone.

When you start questioning what your legacy is and how you could be remembered, you look at your actual accomplishments and how any or all of them can be actually remembered after your death. You then have to question if they are a correct portrayal of how you would want to be remembered.

Many people never overcome their fear of death, simply because they feel there are still so many things they want to accomplish. For me, although additional time would allow me to do even more, I can comfortably say that I have no regrets; I have done and seen some amazing things, both for myself and those around me.

Legacy ties directly into true entrepreneurship, because entrepreneurship is such a lonely road. There are so many unknown variables that make it so hard for just anybody to take the course. Since ideas are unique to each individual, it's impossible for others to bring your business ideas to life. This very unique idea becomes your idea, and reminds you that there is more at stake than just making money: the creation of legacy. This feeling is what enables you to finish what you started despite the obstacles, failures, and more. This feeling is what makes you feel purposeful, empowers you to create the change you envision, and gives you the strength to stand up each and every time you fall. Yet it is nothing more than a false positive, because it is not how your purpose was created. This particular stage in your evolution is how you become curious about what your purpose is. You believe that this new direction you feel in your heart must be what you were born to do. You believe that destiny is the reason your idea is coming to life, and everything else aligns with it. But it is only an illusion. The reality is that the force driving you is your ability to connect the dots for everything that happens and your understanding of the systems that allow you to truly bring your idea to life. This feeling that everything will be OK is nothing more than an enhanced feeling of self-acceptance and self-belief. This feeling of passion is only the beginning of the true journey ahead and a feeling that you will soon never be able to live without.

What you define as your legacy will hold a significant impact on your purpose because as you remember from the First Circle, belief is a combination of education and awareness; therefore, if you define your legacy based on education, then it will help form the belief of your purpose.

Now that you have defined what your legacy looks like, the time has come to embrace the final act of the Third Circle Theory: the removal of yourself from the equation of life.

A Selfless Final Act

Before you make your mark on the world, you must learn that this enduring mark is not about you or your existence — as amazing as that may seem to you — and is indeed a minuscule detail in the big picture of your life. You must learn how insignificant your problems are to the world before you can justify your significance through your actions.

If you died tomorrow, what would be different for the world around you?

The idea of making — and leaving — your mark on the world is not about making everyone remember you, because as we discussed in the first few pages, **the Third Circle Theory is about removing yourself from the equation and not placing yourself in the center of it.** Making your mark is first about deciding what you want to be remembered for, and then being able to find where that fits into the world you live in or the one you want to impact.

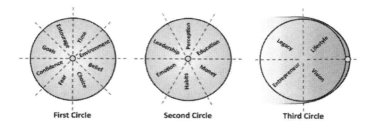

First Circle   Second Circle   Third Circle

In the diagram above, we see that mastering the Third Circle means having the tools necessary to disconnect yourself from your emotions so you can look at the world from a third perspective — one where you mean nothing.

You must be able to accept that the world doesn't revolve around you, and only you can control how you feel about the world and those in it. The circumstances of your life, the places you live, and the society you belong to are nothing more than a fabrication. The feeling of belonging to a religion, group, business, organization, or anything else is one that is created by you and in your control.

It's not a feeling that you consciously fabricated from the experiences, people, and environments you witnessed up to this point. Allowing yourself to comprehend that everything you see around you is the same fabrication through someone else's perspective allows you to understand the depth of all the concepts around you.

You must truly understand that the surrounding you live in is a fabrication of what others deemed necessary to create the society you live in today. From your faith to your beliefs, they are all a reflection of your observations. Think about all those people you observed who also observed others to be the way they are, which means that just about everyone is a copy of someone who has influenced them. If you understand that, then no matter how you feel, think, or what you believe; it doesn't matter, because it is all false. You tend to not understand how it is possible that everything you have been conditioned to see until today is nothing but a creation by others.

Once you get to this stage of disconnect from the world you live in and see reality for what it is (not what you are shown), you start to understand all those concepts we discussed in the circles. You see how our society manipulates everyone in it like a giant game, where all of us play a role. You identify the role you were meant to play, but then choose to no longer play. You realize how quickly someone else replaces your role and the system continues to operate without you. The same occurs when you die; those around you remember you for a few years and the machine of life continues to move on. You may think you genuinely lived a good life, and you will take all your memories with you unless there is a reason for others to remember you. That reason must be that you impacted them or the system they live in on a large enough scale that they will be compelled to remember.

Keep in mind that the majority of the world lives for themselves and their own gain, pleasure, and emotional satisfaction. While you can now say you understand why you shouldn't live selfishly, you also can relate to the fact that people only remember what's important to them.

Removing yourself from the equation is almost like asking the world, "What is it that I can do to serve you?" and finding in those answers, "What ability do I have that matches the needs of the world?"

Doing what I am asking you to do is not easy, and there's a reason that only two percent succeed to become true visionaries. Albeit difficult, the achievement brings you something that 98 percent of the world doesn't have and will never feel truly in their heart and soul, and that is peace

— the peace that if you died tomorrow you could look back and say, "I used my time while alive exactly as I would have wanted to." You have to understand that despite your tenure, wealth, education, and all the other items you accumulated throughout the years, you are no different than the local homeless guy you meet down the street. You are neither richer nor less fortunate than your neighbor who owns a beautiful home.

You are human and just like the rest of humanity, your mark on the world is established through your actions, not your emotions.

When you graduate the Third Circle, you have mastered control over your emotions and understand your place. As you look at life and your environment through a non-emotional lens, you can see the entire picture: the 360°, non-altered, non-edited or manipulated environment in which others live without a clue to all the forces out there driving their decisions, logic, and actions. With this new ability to look at life from a third party perspective, you can identify opportunities much faster and see gaps in the system that you may be able to impact and change. I can agree that the state of mind may not seem like a happy place — possibly a world without much pleasure — but ultimately, it is a place that not only affords you the power to reach beyond what others have accomplished, but enables you to create changes for society and work from a much more significant place than one where money dictates everything. If you live in the Third Circle and graduate past it, you are not without fears but have full control over your fears and the ability to face your emotions.

Think about your friend's poorly managed relationships. Everyone has one of those friends. The two people are unhappy, they fight, and they can never agree on anything. Yet they profess to love each other and stick around. Despite hating each other most of the time, they are unable to separate. No matter which circle you live in, you tend to have an opinion about why they should break up, but they don't realize this because of that emotional block that keeps them from acting — that same block that doesn't exist in this case, because you are not part of the equation. It is much easier for you to say "you should break up," because you don't have to deal with the emotional response and pain that comes with ending a relationship. Even though you are right — they most likely are not a good fit and wasting precious time — they still won't act on this until something bad happens. Until then; however, their first person approach is full of emotions. Your Third Circle perspective doesn't need to see each side of the equation to make a rational decision, because you are exposed to the entire picture at once. You can identify issues more quickly and handle them without much difficulty. If you picture the Third Circle here, you would be looking from the outside into two people in the Circle itself. You're given an edge in identifying a solution by being exposed at once to both people and the world they live in. Your ability to survey an entire situation eliminates the risk of making a rash decision or one that you will later regret.

Being able to provide feedback from a third-person perspective is exactly what the Third Circle Theory is. More importantly, it is not about providing the external influences feedback that you can see (which they can't), but being able to identify your own situations from a third-person perspective rather than your own. This is much more difficult, but if you actually remove your emotions, then you become neutral. You simply analyze information and find the best solutions, regardless of how they make you feel. Seeing the world around you from a third-person perspective makes you realize that there is indeed only two percent of the population who think like you, and the remaining 98 percent can never get past themselves or their emotions. Their lives have no consistency as a result, and they are trapped on an emotional roller coaster that takes them on a tumultuous ride to nowhere.

The key to remaining in the Third Circle and advancing beyond the scope of the 98 percent who wake everyday not seeing what you see is to do the opposite of them; keep your eyes and mind outside of it. By continuing your exploration of society, the world, and all the wonderful things you are exposed to, you now have a very different set of eyes and a very different view of the same picture. I said earlier in this book that you could look at a wallpaper on a glossy smart phone and see the picture it displays. You can appreciate the picture and what it means, but if you look at that picture long enough and through the depth of your vision, you eventually see nothing more than your own reflection in the phone. Even though it's the same item and the same set of eyes, the views are very different based on what your eyes are trained to see. Since your mind now has the information it needs, your eyes will naturally seek this information all around you.

There is no right or wrong, only choice and outcomes when you graduate the Third Circle.

Choice, which is highlighted in the First Circle, looks very different once you graduate the Third Circle. In your earlier years, you make good and bad choices. It is very easy to identify which choices were based on your past perspectives. When you look back after your point of view has changed, the context of choice has morphed as well. It no longer offers two options, such as right or wrong; but only the option of choice itself. In other words, for those of us who control our emotional reactions, then there is no right or wrong anymore and only the choices we make.

If you summed up your life by the choices you made, then you can revisit your life and rethink your past path based on the actions you took. Choice has no right or wrong value, but instead creates an opportunity to take or not take action (lack of action is an action in itself). Even though choice is neutral in nature, the actions we take to support our choices lead to outcomes that are favorable or unfavorable; but nonetheless, in our hands to decide.

This is the mindset Pre-Third Circle:

Success = Good Choices or Failure = Bad Choices

This is the mindset Post-Third Circle:

Choice + Action = Success

There are two important factors when looking at the two equations and what they mean.

1. The Pre-Third Circle equation recognizes the two types of choices and is reflective in nature. People who feel as they do and believe that choices are good or bad usually reflect on their choices after the outcomes have occurred (when it is too late to change them). You see that the result is first and then

followed by the reflection of the outcome. There are also two options, such as success or failure, so there is a clear division between the two choice types.

2. The Post-Third Circle equation tells a different story — only one choice, one option, and one outcome, but action occurs before outcome. Therefore, control of choice is established instead of allowing nature to take its course. There is no reflection of outcome. Instead, change is dictated through action.

The actual equations are not very different from each other. One could argue they reflect the same meaning, which they do, but the Pre-Third Circle puts the person in the passenger seat, while the Post-Third Circle places them in the driver's seat. In the passenger seat you don't control the destination, because you are not acting (driving), only observing, similar to the Pre-Third Circle equation regarding choice. When you eventually understand that as the driver you are in control, then you can choose how to act and where to drive. You have every right to make sure you only stop at the destination you seek. If you choose not to drive, you're able to go where the other 98 percent already went or are going.

Once you graduate the Third Circle, you no longer allow yourself to ride with others. You understand now, better than ever, that no choice is good or bad. It is only a choice with an outcome based on your actions following that choice. You and only you get out what you put in to the choice itself. Let's use starting a business as a great example of how this works.

If you decide to start a business, then many could argue it was either a good or bad choice, depending on whether you get a significant reward or lose everything. For the Pre-Third Circle person who feels that that particular business started was a bad choice, he simply doesn't see that the outcome was in his hands.

Success = Great rewards

Failure = Lose money and time

Now if you live past the Third Circle, then you look at the same situation but add the action piece in the equation. The Post-Third Circle equation looks like this:

Choice (Start a business) + Action (Working very hard and not giving up) = Success (Creating a successful brand)

Another common example is marriage. You can argue that marriage is based on good or bad choices, but the reality has no relevance to that. Here is what that looks like:

Success = Having a Family

Failure = Divorce

Post-Third Circle:

Choice (Getting married) + Action (Finding a compatible someone you also love, as love by itself is an emotion) = Success (Long-lasting relationship)

One can easily say getting married was a poor choice because it's much easier to put the blame on an external factor, but those living past the Third Circle cannot do that. They live their lives by the actions they take after the choice was made, which is necessary to lead it into a favorable outcome. Even in the case that the outcome is not favorable, it still remains the right one, because you learned what doesn't work so that you never repeat the same mistake. Ultimately, there is never a bad choice, only choice itself.

How it Applies in the Real World

Morpheus asked Neo in "The Matrix" movie if he wanted the blue pill or red pill. The blue pill would make you forget anything you just read, and you would wake up every day to the same world you knew before — you may or may not make money and eventually will die happy. By taking the red pill, you would wake up to a world where you would have to fight every day you live to see the truth.

The same can be applied here, as you now have a choice to make. It can be neither good nor bad, but a choice that with action behind it will have an outcome. The choice you have to make is between yourself and others, which can be tricky. You will have to choose who comes first. Understand that you have to detach yourself from others in order to reattach yourself with everyone. The right way is an emotionless decision and much easier said than done.

Imagine that you have to commit an act of generosity that truly inconvenienced you. You would receive nothing at all in exchange. Would you do it?

The way the Third Circle plays in the real world is very similar to this choice because you understand why others do what they do, but they don't understand you. Since mystery is unpredictable, it creates a natural disconnect for people when they run into it. If someone wants to fight you, you find an alternative route of escape instead of provoking the situation further primarily, because the logical step is to not be in a situation that has no positive outcome possible. The hardest part is to identify what those outcomes are in a split second and acting accordingly to the guidelines of the situation. The identification is not just recognizing the impact of your actions on your life, but also looking at the ripple effect of your actions on others and considering their reactions as well. This can prove quite difficult if you are confused by an emotional response to the situation such as fear, anger, hate, jealousy, or just about anything else that can cloud your judgment and action.

Being this way also helps in making sure time is never wasted and that you are acting daily with purpose. You don't just do things to do them; you do them and understand why and how they fit into the bigger picture of your life. This purposeful way of being prompts you to constantly analyze all future possibilities until you eventually piece everything you do together to truly understand how you fit into each particular equation. More importantly, when you combine all these equations you discover where you actually fit in the theory itself.

The real difficulty you are faced with is that you constantly live your life identifying and analyzing risk once you graduate the Third Circle. You are not only focusing on risk as it pertains to you, but its impact on everything else around you as well. You often take risks that you shouldn't when it pertains to helping others, because it puts you at a disadvantage.

For example, I believe my individual purpose is to help others open their eyes to the reality they live in. I used to place myself at significant risk of losing my job, because I pushed the boundaries of leadership with people who couldn't always handle it. Their reactions were predictable, so it was easy to protect myself, but why put myself in that situation to begin with? Ultimately, because the outcome of having one more person choose between the red pill and blue pill was too great to allow my own well-being to prevent me from helping them get to that stage.

That purpose-driven cause is what gives me the strength to detach myself from the fear that risk holds. I am not without fear, but I know how to keep it from manifesting itself so I can move forward rather than doubt my ability to help. Where does all this philosophical stuff lead? What does it all mean?

The Third Circle Theory is not just about helping you wake up and see life's reality; it's a theory that explains why some of you will create empires and

solutions to facilitate the world's greatest challenges, while others create businesses and work a lifetime to make a few bucks. It explains why certain people manipulate the world and why others find ways to help humanity asking for nothing in return. The Third Circle theory also explains life concepts like education, religion, and government; and allows you to see from an unbiased point of view why the world is the way it is and why you are who you are.

It is only when you see in a mirror who you truly are and not who others expect you to be, that you understand what you are capable of and what you can actually accomplish. Once you realize how much control you have over your life and the lives of those around you, you understand where you fit in and what you can do to get there.

When you identify an idea that you want to bring to life, an extraordinary force takes over and gives you the motivation and strength you need to achieve the very completion you envisioned. The entrepreneur in you becomes resourceful — even if you are without any resources — and acts daily until the vision comes to life. All those experiences from the three Circles come together so that you can succeed, but it isn't until you emotionally disconnect from your project that you can truly tap into its potential and allow it to blossom past your expectation.

Why the Self-Help Industry Won't Work

There have been countless books, tutorial videos, and programs all claiming to teach you how to make millions and become successful. Making money isn't related to purpose so despite the desire to grow past the Third Circle, you can remain in the Second Circle, be successful, and make money.

The reality is you can and many do, but not from a video or tutorial; not even proven systems will help you get there, it's up to you. The real problem with the self-help industry is that its teachings, concepts, and attitudes have been diluted by too many programs that are focused on teaching you how to make money. Most people who start self-help businesses are in the game for a quick buck themselves; their intentions with the programs are to help you, but their methods are created in a way that doesn't change your internal behavior, which causes you to give up.

It's almost a Catch-22 if you think about it. In order for you to succeed at all from these systems, you must be in the Second Circle and have mastered the attributes of the First Circle. But in most cases, people in the Second Circle don't need self-help to get them over the hump. They already know how to be successful. It's almost like saying you are catering to a group in the First Circle whom you know will fail; therefore, they will continue to pay for your product because the "Dreamer" stage wants to graduate the First Circle. I have met many self-help gurus in my time, and many of them have had long discussions about their programs. What was most interesting is that the most exciting part of their program is how they monetize it instead of how they help people, which made me question their message.

Here is a great example of why the system will never work as intended. Think of the First Circle people as overweight individuals with bad eating habits, health issues, and lack of fitness. Ask each of them to pick up the latest workout video. The program guarantees losing 10 pounds in three weeks. Three weeks later, it's very likely all of them have lost 10 pounds, which is great. Now here is the trick. Ask them to keep up with the weight loss program for another nine weeks and then check back in with them.

Technically, they should have lost an additional 30 pounds, but you notice that most of them will have not lost more than their original ten pounds. Partly because of their habits and of their environment, which despite the introduction of a solution, simply wasn't enough to sustain the habit. The first ten pounds was easy to lose. They had motivation and drive, because they were being introduced to something new and the mind simply wants to succeed. But when you get past that initial excitement and the rest looks like really hard work, the consistency (habit) wanes. Since the environment hasn't changed (fridge looks the same), a successful outcome never really held a chance.

The reason why shows like *"The Biggest Loser"* are effective is because they remove obese people from their toxic environment, give them a controlled one, and reinforce that environment by having a coach who continues to push for those missing habits, eventually leading to change. The same reasons apply to the self-help industry. It doesn't work because a book can't change your environment or retrain your habits. All it does is awaken the motivation to try, but you haven't learned how to sustain it because you haven't mastered perseverance and drive. You often give up. This is why all these systems start with "If I did it, then so can you…" giving the false assurance to your brain that it's easy. This tease appeals to those who want the easy way out, and in our First Circle that's referred to as the "Dreamer" stage.

Those people in the Second Circle who choose self-help as their focus have often figured out this trick about the First Circle people, and as a result have found a way to monetize it. Nobody but themselves can help people in the First Circle reach the Second through observation, practice, and habits. That is why I wrote this book; people in the First Circle cannot be given a system or solution to moving on in life, but they can be given information to bring awareness to their problems. How you decide to act on it will determine how much farther in life you get. Keep in mind that the road to success — and to graduating from the First to the Second Circle — has been there for decades, yet people still don't follow it. We have factual evidence that smoking will kill you or damage your health, but people still smoke. So it would be foolish to believe that the people in the First Circle will graduate as a result of any system, book, or concept. It was, after all, Edison who said, *"Opportunity is missed by most people, because it is dressed in overalls and looks like work.*"

Most systems out there simply show a map for direction, but the system preys on your inabilities and lack of consistency to give up halfway through. Most self-help programs target people over 30 years of age, partly because they have the means to purchase the program and have lived long enough to form their habits but have yet to succeed. They are the hardest ones to change, because their environment is all they know. They have lived in the First Circle for decades. They lack the behaviors needed to succeed and don't know how to change. The self-help industry provides them hope that a quick change can occur, even though it is much harder for them to break 30 years (or more) of habits.

In order for people to actually help you they must live in the Third Circle, take a great amount of risk by putting themselves out of their comfort zone into yours, and as a result exposing their own vulnerabilities. However, they must stay with you while you change and understand what it takes and which behaviors you need to reinforce before exposing you to the Second Circle. It's very easy to become successful since the road map has been defined a thousand times of how to graduate from the First to the Second Circle. Once the behaviors and environment are tweaked, the change can start to occur and become real. It is ultimately the jump from the Second to the Third Circle that is the hardest. No one can help you make this leap, partly because it is about controlling your inner emotions. There can be nothing but truth between you and your perception of yourself in order to keep moving forward. This book cannot make you graduate the Third Circle; it should help to bring awareness to situations and traits that evoke a response within you. This book is only a manual, and its content is not a means to an outcome, but a trigger to start your journey.

As I mentored people over the years, I came to realize that any book, my writings, or my speeches could never change people. At best, I could trigger change in people. As I graduated to the Third Circle, I realized that if I wanted to reach more people and create a significant change, I had to undertake it one person at a time. That wasn't a good alternative. Instead, I chose to create various tools to help evoke change in people, rather than create yet another map on how to get to that place where you are successful. All of you as individuals — regardless of which Circle you live in or belong to — are successful in your very own ways, and I am not the person to tell you which way to take. My mother never guided me in the right direction, because she also believed in no right or wrong. Instead she educated me on life, so that I could choose my own direction and what it would mean for me. Like her, I'm offering you an ability to look within yourself and then choose if you have lived the life you wanted or the life you were given. If you choose to create a change because you and only you decide that you need to, then I offer you the support through these pages to realize how to create that real change you seek.

How Fulfillment and Purpose are Different

There are people who think they live in the Third Circle but don't. I am referring to those who think that helping people is all about giving them money or a job. You can't buy fulfillment, and you certainly cannot give someone a job that gives you a residual return and expect yourself to be someone who has contributed to society. There is nothing wrong with giving to charity and donating your money for the sake of helping others, but it doesn't put you into the same category as today's great problem-solvers or individuals who do make a difference in society living selflessly.

Donating money creates what I call a false sense of fulfillment — one that doesn't last, which is ultimately why you do it more than once and are not remembered for it. Even if significant in nature, you are only remembered by those directly impacted by the donation itself. How many cancer organizations tell patients being treated that their pills are courtesy of X person who donated to the X foundation? It is often those at the foundation itself that are recognized for their work by society. They are the ones doing the work for you. Even though you feel your donation is needed, it is definitely not the only donation the foundation will receive — and your donation is tax deductible, so you are also benefiting in return. I call this social responsibility, not fulfillment.

True fulfillment comes from having a personal positive impact on someone's life. People need to be helping other people, not their own wallets. Even though you could hire a hundred people to work at a food shelter, people going there to eat won't have the opportunity to be impacted by you, but are impacted by people working the shelter. People who live in the Third Circle are special and empowering. They have charisma and their energy translates to those they touch, who will forever remember the people who helped them. That human interaction of helping another human is what creates true lasting fulfillment, and a bond that is remembered by both people. Imagine you stop on the side of the road and help someone whose tire blew up. You get them back on the road. As small as it is, that gesture is unforgettable because it's not something people do every day. That person in need on the side of the road doesn't know you, understand who you are, or even have interest in helping society will not only forever remember you; but believe me when I say that the person you helped will someday pass that energy forward. It not only feels good to help another person, but it creates connections to others. There is not one person who is better than another, but there are individuals who are more valuable; this value is defined through how many people you help, the experiences you accumulate, and how you live. One of those extraordinary people from society can connect with thousands of people in their lifetime and help them connect with others, but the funny thing is that person living in the Third Circle sees himself as equally valuable as people who have not yet reached the Third Circle.

If you can only get people to invest in their most precious asset — "themselves" — then we can see a much more impactful society that doesn't maintain the selfish "Why should I help you?" mentality. True fulfillment comes from both the connections you make and the positive impact you make with each of those connections; not that false pride you feel for a short while when you donate money in exchange for others to do what you could or should have done.

Understanding Your Value

Someone once asked me, *"What makes one person better than another? Is it money? Power? Education or perhaps intelligence?"*

At first, it was difficult to put a measure of how one person can be considered better than another, because it wasn't clear as to who had the right to actually do the measuring. However, the more I thought about it, the more I broke it down into different aspects of the Circles and why that was such a valid question. Since I am a systematic person and consider myself a businessman, it made sense to look at this question from those perspectives first. I decided to think of it as if I had to choose between two people, how I would value each, and why I would do so.

I thought of it from the measure of money, but felt it was unfair to measure a person's true worth with just pieces of paper. Money is only a small segment of a circle, so it's unreasonable to use it as a valid measurement. I looked at it through the lens of a company first, which applies the measure of someone's worth when they are hiring them —

namely, the salary. That figure is often based upon experience or education, and those two factors enable a company to place a monetary value on someone. A person's ability is ultimately what gets someone hired or not.

From life's point of view, if you take money out of this calculation, then someone's worth is only based upon their understanding of the environment they live in and their ability to survive within it. Therefore, their ability is a common factor of both perspectives. From this point of view, the ability to survive is subjective on environment and your value would diminish or increase based on your environment. You would have one value if you were in the jungle and a different one in a busy city, so the context of ability is subjective based on where you are and the skill set you acquire. Then it leads to your ability to adapt as a new measurement of value.

Ability, skill set, experience, education, adaptation, and the elements mentioned above are all factors that dictate someone's value, yet there is a significant piece still missing - one that is most often missed by employers, businesses, friends, and/or relatives that dictates the true value of a person in any context.

That one single thing is the ability to control your emotions. I think people who can master control over their emotions can accomplish anything they set out to do. That self-control makes them valuable beyond any measure of money, success, or ability. Emotions can make you weak, despite making you human. You can push the boundaries of society and go places others have never imagined possible if you control your emotions. You can stand up to enemies never heard of before and help create the world you wish to live in rather than the one given to you.

That is the way everyone lives in the Third Circle. Their life counts, because they can control it unlike people in the First Circle who, despite having all the same abilities and opportunities, choose to remain who they are and do absolutely nothing other than follow along. As a graduate of life's emotional rollercoaster, you must understand that you have just become significantly more important in society than the average person. Even though you may feel like you are not better than anybody else, you also have to realize that who you are can lead to serious positive changes in this world.

People should know their worth and capacity and must accept their strengths and shortcomings so that they can continue to grow.

Explaining Life's Spider Web

As I mentioned earlier, there are countless systems out there that you will be exposed to as you keep advancing in society — systems that are created to help maintain control and direction for others in society. Banks are a piece of that system, government is another, and there are many more depending on which industry you are looking at. These systems are in place to help facilitate a means of control and ensure that functionality lasts for the long haul. When thinking about the different countries and continents, we can clearly see distinction in which ones have good systems and which have no systems at all. Those with systems that run smoothly and efficiently often times have economies and individuals who are, in most cases, more advanced in their way of living. By "advanced" I'm not referring to smarter, but more in the know and adaptive to the common understanding of the world. These concepts get more complex with time and as societies' needs change. Therefore, they need more and more people to maintain, run, and fund them. No matter which way you look at it, you are part of the systems that make up society, even if you don't like it. The tax system is just one of these systems, for example. Everyone pays taxes that contribute to all these systems, and there is very little escape from taxes. Even if you evade income taxes at the end of the year, you still pay sales or meals taxes when you purchase goods. When you live in the First Circle, you simply don't question these systems. You just abide by them and go on with your life, not questioning the impact they have or don't have on your life. You don't attempt to understand them, because you feel there is nothing you can do to change it, even if you tried or complained. People either gain or lose confidence in government when things like gas prices, unemployment, or finance rates increase for the worst. You believe that the government controls these systems and that voting is your power to fight back when unhappy. Those who live in the Second Circle on the other hand, don't really care about the systems in place, but instead choose to understand the depth of how they work in order to benefit themselves. Those who make more money pay fewer taxes, because they know how to not pay taxes by spending more money where it matters. They become experts in this field or pay others to do that for them. Their understanding of the system allows them to manipulate its inner workings just enough so that no one notices while still benefiting them.

It was people in the First Circle who destroyed this country during the 2006-2008 housing crash. Their focus on making money by trying to flip homes without understanding the depth of what was involved made them vulnerable to predatory lending. People in the Second Circle figured out the tricks to making the real estate system work in their favor when purchasing multiple homes and flipping them. While they were after money and knew the tricks to the government programs and the financial system, those in the First Circle didn't. As a result, those buyers were taken advantage of by those systems in the same way that the Second Circle homebuyers had accomplished. It was the fear of missing out on making money that hurt First Circle investors when they tried to duplicate what was happening in their environment. First Circle individuals don't understand these concepts; all they see are the outcomes. Instead of leveraging those systems, First Circle people simply contributed to them. They were outsmarted by the manipulators in the Second Circle. Ultimately, it was the First Circle individual's lack of attention and care that caused their own downfall. Since 80 percent of the population lives in the First Circle, that resulted in a lot of people falling. Those who live in the Second Circle either got out early or positioned themselves to leverage the crash.

Third Circle individuals, on the other hand, also can take advantage of systems and concepts, but don't feel that they need to. Instead, they see where there are missing pieces and find ways to either create a better system or protect those who don't understand them by helping to educate or designing programs to protect First Circle individuals. The ability to understand and see the entire design of these systems is what differentiates those in the Third Circle from those in the Second. While people in the Second Circle see how concepts and systems benefit them, people in the Third Circle see how concepts and systems operate, and thus improve or fix them.

Regardless of which Circle you live in, you are naturally involved in a few systems that are too big to avoid. They are broken into government, corporate America, and education. At some point, you are not only exposed to these systems, but are entangled in their web. I am going to break down each of these and show you how they are keeping you from moving past the Third Circle, but more importantly, why they are keeping you back.

The Entrapment of Society

Society as a whole is a system that is operated and maintained by individuals with a common set of beliefs or values. Despite being one society, we are broken down into sub-societies (which we refer to as geographical states). Based on our values, beliefs, and needs we can choose which appeals to us most.

Society has a weird way of maintaining itself by allowing you to create the balance it needs. Everyone is different, depending on where and how you are born and/or reside today. Think of society as a giant spider web, and all those matrix-like web connectors to be components like education and corporate America. The reason I compare society to a giant spider web is because the spider web does its best to keep you glued in one place, rather than explore the world. The web likes it when you play nice within the sticky strands, and not outside of it. This giant spider web is complex and as you move forward in life, it gets more and more complex to support itself. As a result, you must educate people on how to operate within it.

"Within it" are the key words here, as the system requires each of you to play a part inside of it. Some of you need to be construction workers, others need to be doctors and lawyers — all of you are constantly feeding and advancing the same system to grow larger and run better. The system offers multiple lines of support to ensure that your aspirations and observations lead to your contribution to society. Then the system provides support to ensure you get there. If you choose to take a road that has yet to be paved, you are there alone but can be rewarded significantly because your work (if you succeed) will pave the way for others to now weave into the spider web known as society. It all starts from your earlier years in school. The idea isn't to reject the system but to understand it.

The Role of Education

Education plays an important role in making sure you stay in the First or Second Circle. Most of what we consider formal, school-based education is preparing us to survive in a conventional First Circle way; conforming to the guidelines of society and doing its best to keep you in line to becoming a contributing member by the time you leave the classroom environment. Think about high school, as an example. Most of the career counselors guide you towards a job, not so much owning your own business or becoming an innovator, but just doing your part in the bigger picture. Society needs doctors, lawyers, engineers, technicians, and business managers to keep things running efficiently, and it's the role of the early education system to put in your head that those other dreams of owning businesses, innovating the world, or thinking outside the box are not typical successful routes to take. Have you ever wondered why that is? Why does this behavior also continue into less accredited colleges and community colleges? Why does everyone want to teach you a skill to work for others? Why is it that only Ivy League schools seem to put out inventors, innovators, and great business minds? Is it the education they provide?

All of those are great questions, and the answer is the people producing the content. Entrepreneurship is something that most Ivy League schools are very familiar with because they hire retired executives, retired business figures, and other innovators and free thinkers to teach their classes and courses. This gives their students the exposure they need to understand that there is a high probability of success. In other colleges, entrepreneurship simply isn't carried with the same weight due to the ratio of those teaching those skills. It's almost like breaking down and saying you can have a mentor who has done it or a mentor who has studied it; even though education is great, it is not a substitute for experience no matter in what context.

The role of education is to prepare you for society and being a functional piece of a working machine. It has very little tolerance for people who choose to build their own machine and don't want to conform to the system's standards. It wasn't until the last two years that schools started advertising entrepreneurship as a major because of its need to conform to what society is doing. Think about how the perception is that with a degree you are guaranteed a good salary, but without it you are not. That misconception has been around for so many generations that parents force college on their kids who don't even know why they have to go. Why would you invest all this money and time into a piece of paper someone may never use?

It is the role of every one of these teachers trapped in the First Circle themselves to show you how conventional education and employment leads to a successful life, and that the more time you spend in school getting advanced degrees, the more likely you are to make a lot of money. Because their lives are about survival and the money they make, your observations are what they reinforce over and over again. What's even funnier is how government supports this concept.

The Role of Government

Government is another way to encourage one action over another, making it even more difficult for you to choose your own way out. Think about the support that government gives to conventional education with student loans, grants, and rewards just for choosing to go to school. This institution is simply looking out for itself to continue functioning. The sooner you go to work, the sooner you pay taxes, and the sooner you contribute labor to society. More importantly, **it entraps you by loading you down with debt from a very young age,** which makes you dependent on work in order to avoid financial ruin early on. This is one of the many ways the government pushes you towards belonging to the system. It's only when there is a flaw in its system — like job scarcity — that the government acts as though it's helping others create more machines to help the masses function.

Outside of its interaction with education, government also goes out of its way to keep people spending and borrowing more. It leverages man's greatest emotional asset — money — to keep you in your place. Debt is the government's weapon to make sure you constantly live in fear of losing your job, so it leverages access to money to keep feeding itself while at the same time making you believe it's helping you. The government itself is one giant business, and you are its most valuable asset; therefore, the more you think about stepping out of its cycle or understanding how it works, the more it leverages media to make you feel like an outcast.

As much as we can hope for a society where the private sector controls and governs all types of trade and regulation, that will never happen — partly because people are too self-centered and greedy. Only two percent live past the Third Circle; the other 98 percent are out to get what they deem to be their rightful share. That greed is so powerful that it can break up families and businesses, and even lead to crime. This lack of separation from the emotional need of always having more money creates a constant battle to keep people fighting for themselves. It isn't until a greater common enemy comes along and scares us even more than not having money that we unite.

As human beings, we are constantly full of emotions and often allow our emotions to dictate our character. We feel a certain way about people, races, backgrounds, and ways of life, but we allow how we feel to dictate how we act. It is a reality we unfortunately face, a reality where we judge everyone around us by where they are born, what they believe in, and what color their skin is. But how much of our beliefs are actually our own, and how much come from where we are born and the color of our skin? Would you hate someone who was born in a different hospital than yours, but was just down the street? Would you do wrong to someone at work making more than you by 50 cents?

You probably answered no to both of those questions; but despite saying no, we have such a strong feeling of discomfort with people who are not like us. The main reason is because as emotional human beings, we allow our emotions to decide how we act rather than our logic, which should be understood as to why people are as they are. We don't hate or have emotions towards those down the street in a different hospital, or those at work making more than us because we understand why and who they are. On the other hand, we don't understand other people in different countries. We don't understand the poor people who live in third world countries, and we don't understand the misery of people living under dictatorships.

Our lack of understanding and care for understanding is what makes us divided and incapable of creating true impactful change in the world. We don't care for that change because we believe we are happy, even though in most cases, we actually are not. We are simply grateful to be who we are and have what we have. We choose to look the other way instead of getting to know and understand those who might one day need our help. So in happiness, we remain divided. A division that grows deeper as the world continues; a division of people, race, religion, and more…

There is; however, a common feeling that brings us together every time, a feeling that is common for 100 percent of the planet even though some control it better than others. This feeling is the emotion known as *fear*.

Fear is what keeps people from being great. It is the emotion that keeps those wanting to achieve from trying, and those wanting to love from liking; but it is nonetheless a common emotion that everyone on earth has felt or will feel at one point or another. Think about every bad event that has occurred around you, from attacks on our way of life, to leaders creating policies that destroy this country, and even accidents and acts of violence around us. It is fear that makes everyone come together to create change. It is fear that makes everyone come outside their homes to gather around a shooting. It is fear that makes people who usually don't vote, care to vote, and it is fear that makes people want to know others they previously didn't care for. It is the common emotion that allows us to act in a state where the mutual interest is the best option.

But why does it have to be this way? I challenge everyone reading this today to go out just one day this week and do something nice for someone you don't know (expecting nothing in return). I challenge you to try to get to know the person you did something for and understand what makes them amazing in their own way. Some will actually not let you do anything for them; others will reject you not even knowing you and ask why you are being generous to them. If you can make a change in one person's life this week and try to understand someone else that you would have never gotten to know otherwise, then you have helped humanity take one step forward away from fear.

For that guy who feels like saying, "What is one act of generosity going to do to change the world?" I want you to remember that every major event in this world had to start small at some point by one person, one idea, and one action. That person can and should be YOU.

The private sector also has its own means of control and works very well with government once it reaches a certain size. Most large businesses work side by side with the government to not only benefit personally, but also because the government is now obligated to rely on their commerce. Whether it's direct involvement with government affairs — like defense contracting, banking, and automotive manufacturing — or because the amount of money they generate impacts the government significantly in its own revenue and employment numbers. But how does it all work together?

The Role of Corporate America

When you work for a company, it's in that company's best interest to keep you there, ensuring that the slightest idea you may have of going out of the box and seeking employment elsewhere or pursuing your dreams is reinforced by their talk of uncertainty. Working for others from an early age is great because there is quite a lot to learn, but it is also one of the main reasons people don't follow their dreams. You become comfortable and secure. It's just easy. No matter the nature of your work, practice makes perfect and your abilities become better with time. That is exactly what a company wishes to happen: for you to become an expert in your field so that you become disconnected with what's going on and even more comfortable with staying where you are. The emotional role that corporate America plays is simply to get you comfortable and secure with not only an income larger than one you'll make the first three years of working for yourself, but also the security of knowing you can count on a regular paycheck and take on debts. This then creates this domino effect of obligations preventing your from taking risk. Think about why most people say, "You've got to do it while you are young." That is because obligations — like your spouse, kids, debt, and the inability to take risks — all become firmer with time and make it harder for you to have the energy to fight all the forces up against you at an older age.

The education system, government, and corporate America are by no means evil; nor do they need to be removed or changed. The President is not going to be the one making every change to make everything better. It is you who can make the changes needed. You can make sure you don't overspend and become part of this never-ending trap that that nine out of ten people fall into. You, as individuals, can make sure you understand your own values and that education does not have to be limited to the confines of a classroom. It comes from your observations of people you wish to be like and those who offer to mentor and help you.

You even have a very easy way to break away from this false security that corporate America gives you. You have the ability to break your comfort zone every few years, just so you can continue to reach new heights and be exposed to new environments. Here is how you can do that if you want to reach self-actualization.

Break Your Comfort Zone by Creating Change

You might be saying that all of this talk of Circles is great, but how can you really control your journey if all information is not always true? That is a very valid question and worth taking the time to discuss.

Have you ever wondered why immigrants work harder than Americans in the United States? Their understanding, appreciation for opportunity, and hard work is a strong motivator. Where did this appreciation come from? The appreciation came from not having that same resource at home and understanding that when presented with it, it must be cherished and taken advantage of.

Here is a look at how evolution is based on the perspective of observation as well as the observation itself. Have you ever looked at the same item at two different times in your life and felt entirely different about it? Toys are a great example of that. When you were a child, you wanted more toys because your observations were highly focused on toys. As you grew older and realized the value of certain toys, you looked at them with less desire and perhaps no longer even cared to own them. That is because your personality changes, and your priorities change along with it. You look at certain things in different ways. Despite the fact that you might still appreciate a butterfly, its colors and flying patterns meant more the first few times than they do today. Your lack of observations gave more value to each and everything you observed. This is why children observe faster than adults, because they have seen very little, so any little thing can leave a lasting impression. Those impressions often fade with time as more and more information is processed. Certain information loses its value as past observations were made and the beliefs of the person changed.

These observations lose their value the same way in real life. The more comfortable you are with what you see, the less alert and interesting it becomes. Think about French people and the Eiffel tower. They aren't as excited about visiting the site as tourists are, but they are thrilled to go to the Empire State Building. Your curiosity comes from observations, followed by the desire to understand what you see. The more you see something, the less curious you are, and the less interested you are in seeing it.

As a child, you do not hold the option to choose what you see or how you see it, because you don't understand how to interpret anything you see. As you get older, your observations are much more impacted by your beliefs than by your eyes. You see not only what you believe, but also what you understand. A lot can be said of those same immigrants above who came here for opportunity, because they have seen a lack of opportunity early on in life and appreciate the chance of success presented to them later on. Employment in other countries is not as accessible and easy as it is in the United States. Even with a 10 percent unemployment rate, the US still has opportunities for everyone, while other countries fail significantly. This observation of all these difficulties allows immigrants to appreciate the ease of getting what they couldn't acquire before.

For instance, as a child growing up in France, I witnessed my mother become an entrepreneur because employment wasn't easy to come by. So early on I realized the importance of working, which made me feel the immediate need to get a job at 14-years-old. Seeing how people lived in France and how scarce moneymaking opportunities were, I embraced the power of having access to work and the ease of being entrepreneurial here. I also witnessed the fear of an unbalanced government in the Middle East and appreciated the freedom and rights that came with living in the United States. As a result, I investigated and exercised my rights when we moved here, but never took them for granted. My earlier observations were forced on me and didn't give me the opportunity to interpret them in any way except one — through the lens of my mom's beliefs. As you grow older and choose what you see like I did, you tend to miss a lot because you are naturally egocentric and only observe items that are relevant to you. If you like fashion, then you notice what people wear in other countries. You don't, for example, investigate people's retirement funds and how they differ. You focus your time on things that interest you, which is why the best time to make your children see other countries is when they are young and can absorb all information, not just one type based on your beliefs or observations.

If every child visited two different countries between the ages of 9 and 12, they would definitely be more cultured, understanding, and capable. At that age, they still absorb everything and understand the context of society.

As you get older; however, the world around you changes. Things like your job and family keep you planted in one destination, which significantly impacts your environment and growth. As we discussed earlier, your observations become dull and you miss most of what's around because of the routines you exercise and passive viewing you hold. This brings on comfort and plays a big role in keeping you complacent, since it comes from the routine of observation. The more you observe the same thing, the less it interests you and pushes you to learn more, and as a result, failing to act in your environment kicks in. Since there is no need to take action in your environment, you simply don't care.

The same situation can be applied to your relationship with a loved one. The honeymoon stage in a relationship occurs because things are new and everything is interesting, but as you grow tired of the same visual, situations, or problems, you no longer pay attention or try to impress the person. You drift into a routine. This becomes very apparent when kids are introduced into the picture, as they facilitate that routine and actually make it harder to break out of it. The couples who accept the most change in their relationship tend to last longer. From employment change to constant travel together, the change in scenery and environment breaks the routine and allows freshness, even if it's not directly correlated to the couple. Laziness and routine can keep you from changing Circles and never help you discover what your life could be. Instead, you always wonder. This is where most people experience a midlife crisis. That same routine applies to where you live. The more comfortable and the less interesting it is, the more routine your behavior in that city or town.

Laziness and comfort are common issues that impact a large number of people, but there is a cure for those who can harness their fears enough to create the change they seek. This change occurs by taking a chance in changing your environment, which is necessary if you wish to break your routine.

Here is a method I use to break out of my own plateau or routines. Every four to five years, I create change to force myself to be uncomfortable — change my state, job, country, or home; whatever it takes to change my perspective and get out of my comfort zone. This shift then makes me alert to new observations. I'm forced to make changes to my life in order to accommodate this new environment. Give it a try! You ultimately help yourself and those around you to see more than they may ever have seen in that so-called honeymoon stage. When you grow older and this change is self-created rather than forced, be strategic about what you are looking at to observe and create the specific change you seek.

Think about the fish in the pond. You start as a small fish in your pond. Eventually, you grow and become the larger fish in the pond by becoming familiar with the pond and everything in it. You can choose to remain that fish and live in that small pond — dominating small fishes — or you can accept that if you were to move to a larger pond, you wouldn't be considered large anymore. You become the smaller fish once more. This would force you to learn more to survive in this larger pond. The size of the fish (you) never gets bigger with time; however, you put yourself in a situation that forces you to grow more. Think about the same fish after traveling through four different large ponds. It would no longer fit into that first pond anymore, even if at the beginning that fish felt large.

I was a small fish when I started working in Washington, D.C. but quickly grew to become the larger fish; one of the few people driving exotic cars at a young age and living well enough to be recognized as a big fish by others. Once I was acknowledged as such, it almost became routine to be appreciated, so that acknowledgment lost its value because people valued only my possessions. As a result of being a big fish, I questioned if perhaps my pond was large enough for me to keep growing.

Since it wasn't, I positioned myself to go and live in Boca Raton, Florida because I knew it was one of the largest concentrations of wealth in the world. I changed my pond to one of the largest out there, which immediately reduced me to a very small fish once more. People in Boca Raton had wealth beyond what those people in DC could comprehend, and they lived in a very different fashion as well. I went from a working city to a wealth-based, retirement city. That changed not only my pond, but also the dynamics of how that pond worked. This entirely broke my routine and my comfort zone, but allowed me to grow significantly more. My observations were so significantly different from one city to another that I can honestly say that going to back to DC almost makes me feel invincible, because I now realize how small I was there — making me able to now be more humble because my value has been defined differently now that I see what possibilities are out there. This change in perspective is an immense lesson for me.

These types of changes are not easy, but very necessary if you wish to actually move to a state of control over your emotions. Remember that we are not judged by who we are, but our actions through time and their impact on others. Putting yourself at stake only allows you to make fear the routine, which is fine since you want fear to become part of your life so you can control it much easier than most because you've experienced it before. Put yourself at stake until you no longer feel you are, even though your routines continue. In this way, you create a repetition that allows you to rely solely on yourself and your ability, and eventually you venture places others fear to visit. The better you get, the more you become aware of your environment rather than remain lost in your fears of survival.

Living for the Experience of Life Itself

When you learn to foster and harness your emotions, you see all of life's designs as ordinary as others see their home. It is imperative that once you reach the Third Circle, you understand your value in life and comprehend that life has a grand design. There is a lot of beauty in things that may seem ordinary to other people. The finance system, as an example, is looked at as evil because it exists to take people's money if looked at from the First Circle viewpoint. Those in the Third Circle see that this was at one point nothing more than someone else's vision. It now powers how we live. It ultimately is no different than the innovation of the light bulb, and while it may be true that plenty of people in the Second Circle learned how to make the system work for themselves, you can appreciate this major creation for what it is. You understand how it can be tweaked to benefit everyone instead of only funding one person.

Regardless of what systems you impact and what amazing systems you discover in life, it all starts with your observations, which are now very different than before. These observations are almost an admiration for the way things function and prosper, not just looking at the final outcome. Your ability to continue your observations from this very new perspective is part of the process in finding where you fit into the equation. You can help create innovation without understanding what exists all around you and how it currently works.

Your observations now mean more than ever before, as both your eyes and your brain understand them. My only advice to you is to ensure that you continue to explore life by constantly exposing yourself to new elements. Make sure you take a second to enjoy all the visuals that the world has to offer, especially when appreciated for their design and not so much their beauty.

The continued experience of life itself is another advantage of living in the Third Circle, as you now start experiencing what living really is. You no longer worry about just your existence. You understand that defining your existence occurs through the action you take living life to the fullest and impacting others positively. You understand that simply going to work each and every day doing the same thing without understanding why is no longer an option.

If there are two things you should take away from the Third Circle Theory, it is that the world doesn't revolve around you and actions, not thoughts, define who we are. There should never be a time when you allow other people's actions to prevent you from acting on your own, and definitely not a time when you allow circumstances outside of your control to stop your actions. There can be no victory and no change without action. **Living life to the fullest is about having control over your outcomes and** understanding that nothing can stop you from enjoying everything around you, except yourself.

The Birth of Purpose

The self-help industry as a whole doesn't work and as we discussed earlier, the same reasons apply to the workout videos. The problem is not that the information is inaccurate or repetitive, but the fact that they want you to change behaviors in your life in order to get to the goal often defined as "getting rich." That goal is not important; it's subjective to perspective. Your behaviors are not aligned with your goals, but the reason you haven't made enough money is also because of how you think about what you do. The habits you need to have established in order to be able to be successful are not there either.

The only issue at hand here is that everything you do is based upon one factor only — self-gain. No matter how good the self-help program or the information is, their underlying idea is to create something that ultimately benefits them more than you. If their program does benefit you, that's great. But if it doesn't, they don't care. The reason why the self-help industry has a bad reputation is because it is, in most cases, about their own gain even though their sales message is about helping you. It simply comes across as fraud once the success rate of the product is not favorable for the masses. "Rich Dad, Poor Dad" was a phenomenal book and full of good ideas, but the programs offered beyond the book were meant to generate income rather than help people. The seminars became more expensive and taught by people without merit. Slowly, people caught on and walked away from the weak opportunity it was presenting.

People who succeed often don't want to share information, because they don't need more money so sharing information, writing a book, or helping others isn't their primary concern. This doesn't describe everyone, but a large segment of people.

Then there is the privacy issue. Despite trying to help others, the self-helpers often feel as though putting themselves out there doesn't result in anything for them besides exposing their personal business that might hurt them at some point. There are also those people who never really made any money but have spent their entire lives telling others fake stories that could jeopardize their integrity if made public. There are so many obstacles keeping those with true stories from sharing that almost makes it more difficult to get a good message out there, unless so many layers benefit before the end user actually can.

Think about this: no two paths are identical, and no existing path holds the same reward for the follower as it does for the innovator and builder. That hope, nonetheless, is what keeps people following others. The hope that the reward will be worthwhile with minimal effort is what prevents people from ever graduating the First Circle and causes others to take advantage of that weakness for money.

If you hold everything true that you discovered during your journey to the Third Circle, then you know that information is neutral. Your feelings toward the information doesn't matter but the information itself does. In the effort to grow, you must expose yourself to observations in order to trigger your desire to seek more information. When the path to defining yourself isn't obvious, it's not because it doesn't exist, but that you have not yet seen it to create the information you need about it. For example, just because a road is only two lanes wide doesn't mean that three lanes cannot exist. It just means that no one has built a third lane yet. You have the same opportunity to envision and build the road that others cannot see. You will then enjoy the rewards at the end before anyone else can travel down the same path. It is imperative that you create a road that others can also discover and travel through, because that is how we grow as a society. If you are constantly seeking other paths to follow, then you are merely creating income, not innovation.

Think about your life today as it stands, and think about all the experiences, observations, and accomplishments that have made you who you are. Think about how many people you've been able to touch, inspire, and help in your lifetime, no matter how long you've been here. Think about the unpredictable world we live in, and how quickly things can end for anyone. Now ask yourself this:

"If I died tomorrow, what would people remember me for?
And who outside of my immediate family and friends would
tell my stories to others?"

Take a second to reflect on that. Ask yourself if the money you constantly chase, the choices you make strictly because of money, and the destinations you choose each day truly are a reflection of how and what you want people to remember you by. If so, then continue on. But if you decide that you have not been working towards the right goals, then the time to revisit and change directions is now. Not tomorrow, not next week, not next year, but today. Ask yourself if you would rather wait around ten years only to find out what you could have accomplished, or would you rather look back in ten years and remember the great experiences and amazing people you met along your journey while building your legacy?

Oscar Wilde said, "To live is the rarest thing in the world. Most people just exist." Those who don't live life for the experience but exist only for the outcomes are missing out. They have the opportunity to change their outcome and their experiences through the choices and actions they take each and every second they exist.

What society really needs to affect true change is a voice, an unaltered real and unbiased voice that can only speak truth — even if it's uncomfortable at times. A voice that doesn't take credit for creating change, but takes any shape it needs to manifest the change and bring a higher level of trust amongst each other. A voice that knows fear and when to control it, so that it can still be heard. This voice is your voice; and unfortunately, it will have no merit until you believe it does. Your voice is the most important factor to creating the change you seek and helping in your quest to bring back the true meaning of entrepreneurship. All of you have the skill set and talent within you. All you need is to believe that this gift exists, and it becomes possible to travel where others have not.

The Birth of an Idea

Entrepreneurship is about vision, creation, and innovation. It's a way of life and a way of living. In the past decade, entrepreneurship has lost its true meaning and prestige. Instead, it has been looked at as a synonym for being "self-employed." There was a time when entrepreneurs were admired for their guts, courage, and innovative thinking for undertaking some of life's biggest challenges and solving them for the benefit of those around them. This selflessness that made entrepreneurs who they are and gave them their identity in the world has devolved into nothing more than a rat race of competitors trying to prove who has or can make the most money. The world of entrepreneurship has been invaded by false opportunities. True entrepreneurs are not defined by how much money they've made, but by the innovations they create and the impact they make on others around them. Those who tell you they are entrepreneurs when they have learned to master a skill that enables them to make money are fooling themselves. **A true entrepreneur sees the world for what it can be, not for what it is currently**. Even though there is a significant reward for their efforts when they see a task to the end, a true entrepreneur's drive and passion never revolves around the reward, but the journey itself and the birth of innovation.

Having created innovation or attempting to do so does make someone an entrepreneur, even if there has been no reward in a monetary sense. There are entrepreneurs who are more skilled than others, and some who are more experienced than others, but that doesn't define the importance of one's self. Those who are more skilled have grown both their skill set and mindset to rise up to the challenge to create innovation. They give birth to an idea and along the way have learned to deal with failure, which allows them to get closer to a solution. Those entrepreneurs understand that the thrill of bringing an idea to life is about overcoming failures and being able to move past your emotions into a state of selflessness. The reason entrepreneurship has become misrepresented and is now a synonym for self- employment is because corporate America and major organizations across every industry have found a way to rob entrepreneurs of their ideas with money — money that although is necessary, has changed the meaning of entrepreneurship forever. People now create companies only to sell them to others, instead of helping those around them. They now take the time to create businesses to teach others how to make money in order to make money themselves, knowing that few people will ever succeed. The true meaning of entrepreneurship has significantly lost its meaning from the Thomas Edison and Walt Disney days; but it doesn't have to continue on this downward spiral, and we can change that.

We can learn to put our differences aside, our past observations and beliefs behind, and find a way to reconnect true entrepreneurs together so that real innovation and change can take place all around us. More importantly, we as entrepreneurs can show those around us the true meaning of selflessness. To live for the greater good of humanity rather than our own personal satisfaction may seem like a lot to ask, but it can have a significant impact on the world.

Secret Entourage is more than a website, a book, or a dose of motivation. It is an attempt to bring back what entrepreneurship once was and to enable those who truly understand, embrace, and live the life of an entrepreneur to have a place to come together and hold each other accountable. At the same time, we grow our own talents by learning and observing from one another, and being in a position to help one another create the much-needed change our society needs. If you believe that there has to be more to this life than just how much money you can make, that we were not created to spend our whole lives pursuing a piece of paper, and that our actions towards one another define the person we become, then join me in this quest to give back and help others see what we see. People deserve to know that their life doesn't have to be ordinary, and that their circumstances do not have to dictate their outcome. They must understand that even if others do not feel the same, an act of generosity can go a long way.

Secret Entourage is not about hiding your identity when helping others, but understanding that anyone who believes in true entrepreneurship can have a voice regardless of their age, social status, or the amount of money they have made. Anyone can have a great idea and be a driver for change or a leader rather than a follower. Anyone with the desire to succeed should have the help and support of those around them, so that in return they can one day help others do the same.

My vision of what the world should be is the reason I believe Secret Entourage is needed, and why I spend all my energy, resources, and time making sure that this venture can succeed and become the platform that entrepreneurs use to push ahead past the obstacles that our circumstances and past choices have led us to. My greatest skill set has always been to help people — not by showing them what to do, but knowing them better than themselves and enabling them to understand who they are and who they wish to be, and then offering them the tools and support to allow them the change they seek. Over the past ten years, I have helped people realize that their present situation doesn't have to dictate their future outcome, and that every choice they make can change what happens tomorrow. Many have succeeded, but others simply gave up and enjoyed their way of life even if they chose to remain a by-product of their environment and focus on themselves. However, I can tell you that every one of those people who I helped did find in themselves the answers to what their purpose was and made sure that their impact on society and those around them was as powerful as the impact I had on them.

From my earliest age to present day, I have observed a woman give her entire life, devotion, and everything she had for the well-being of her child, despite all odds and obstacles in her way. She always chose the harder way for herself if it would make her son's life easier. She has traveled continents without money, sacrificed her health and comfort so that her child could live comfortably. I sometimes question what force or energy allows such selfless acts, and what goes on in the minds of people capable of such acts. I then understood that such selflessness couldn't be repaid by any amount of money or any amount of success. It can only be paid forward by touching the lives of many others in the same sense.

Many will call me insane for thinking I can bring this change to the world and get people to become more aware of other people instead of always focusing on themselves. I am not expecting my efforts to change humanity or alter the course of history. One man cannot change the world, but he can ignite a spark in others that will eventually create the change he wishes to see. If I gave up on helping others because of those who see no value in what I do, or those who simply have no trust in others and feel there must be another reason why I choose to help them, then I wouldn't be true to my very own beliefs and wouldn't be living in the Third Circle. It is my ability to believe in this possibility more than I believe in my own existence that allows me to continue inspiring change in people with the same energy and passion I had when I first started.

If you wake up feeling like you are worth more than what you do today, then take the time to understand where you are lacking in your own growth. Be honest with yourself and find a way to reach your very own Third Circle. Once you get there, you will see how powerful its residual effect really is. It will allow you to find a new meaning for why you exist, just like it did for me. There is no way to physically prove at any time that what you believe to be your purpose ever was or ever will be, but it's irrelevant because the energy that your belief produces and its impact on those around you will be so significant that it will give a new **meaning to how you live life**. It is, after all, people like us who remember us, tell our stories, share our pictures, and share how we impacted their lives. It is other people who validate our existence.

Final Words

I hope you have enjoyed reading the Third Circle Theory, and at the very least, absorbed information that will help you redefine yourself and find the true meaning of your very own life.

I've had the privilege of having some extraordinary influences and people around me, all of whom have made me who I am today. I want to take a moment to recognize them for their selflessness and their contributions to my life.

First of all, my mother Shahla, a beautiful woman who devoted her life to working and sacrificed everything so that I could live my life freely. Your devotion to our survival and your support throughout all these years were not for nothing. After understanding how and why people become who they are, it is only natural that I am a perfect reflection of you. It is because of the sacrifices you made throughout the past 30 years that I am able to take the next step in helping people while truly honoring your name, character, and well being. There is no battle or past circumstance I regret, and there is no better mother than the one who chooses her own child over herself each and every time. I could not be more proud of you and your accomplishments, but more importantly, I could have never asked for a better mother than you. Thank you!

Navid and Alan — two extraordinary individuals who devote their most precious resources and time to help bring a vision to life: a vision that can help others realize what they are missing out on when it comes to living. These outstanding people have every chance to be selfish and focus on many money-making opportunities that could give them all the wealth and materialistic possessions one desires, but instead they believe in people enough to devote their time and energy to something that is not about them, but about those around them. Their drive, passion, and powerful work ethic are second to none. Their loyalty and love for people they have never met and the impact they are making in a selfish society reminds me each and every day that our work matters, and that our destination is none other than the one we envisioned. The experience of working with such an incredible team is truly a privilege, one that I wish more people could experience, but also one that has made me a much better person as a result. The work you guys have done is truly remarkable, and I am very excited for the things to come in the next 10 years and also seeing our friendship evolve.

I also want to recognize my Uncle Parviz, who established himself as a leader, coach, father, and mentor for me growing up and who, despite sharing a very different outlook on life, stood behind me in every time of need. Your selflessness, generosity, and devotion to others are exemplary and played a significant role in my upbringing and success. Thank you for being there when it mattered.

I also want to thank Ahmad, a mentor in my finance career who showed me that taking chances on people based on who they are—not just what they've done—and helping them reach their potential is what fulfillment is all about. He once took a chance on me because of who I could become and not what I looked like on paper. His commitment to investing his time in others without ever expecting anything in return is a reflection of the true meaning of generosity.

Thank you to all those who allowed me to be their mentor during times of uncertainty and gave me their trust and loyalty when I needed it the most. Great leaders are only as good as the people they lead, and I can proudly say that I led some of the most incredible people throughout my different roles and projects. Your sacrifices and unconditional support will never be forgotten.

Public figures like Henry Ford, Bill Gates, Walt Disney, Steve Jobs, and many others who remained true to their cause and made their mark in history, even if at times they never got to enjoy the fruits of their hard work. Their words, actions, and dedication to something greater than themselves makes them the true pioneers of the Third Circle Theory and reinforces my belief everyday that we are only as good as our actions and our ability to help others along the way. Thank you for showing everyone that if you dream it, then you can do it!

I want to also thank all of the people who didn't believe in Secret Entourage and provided the opposition and obstacles that I needed in order to find out what I was made of. All your efforts to stop me, hold me down, and prevent me from being all I could be allowed me to gain the strength, courage, and mindset to overcome any objections or fears that has come my way. Without your limited thinking and mediocre way of living, I would have never been able to recognize what defines an extraordinary person and would have never been able to differentiate the sweet from the sour in life.

Last but not least, thank you to all of the fans, readers, followers, and members who email our team each and everyday, reminding us of the impact we have made in their lives and the inspiration and guidance we provide. Your words, letters, and emails mean a lot to every member of our team, and you give us the fuel we need to validate that our work matters. Thank you for your loyalty, support, and generosity in bringing awareness to all we do.

About The Author

Pejman Ghadimi is a self-made entrepreneur and best selling book author born in 1982 in the middle of a revolution in Iran. He was raised in France for the majority of his childhood, and eventually immigrated to the United States in 1997. Raised by a single mother his entire life with very limited resources, Pejman quickly adapted to the idea of being resourceful. Due to the lack of finances, Pejman chose to start working at a young age and focused his efforts on finance where he was able to build a name for himself very quickly. He was able to climb the ladder all the way to the VP level in a short four years all without any type of formal education. Fast forward three more years, Pejman decided to leave banking with a significant amount of experience, which was later applied to founding three major businesses: VIP Motoring, Secret Consulting, and Secret Entourage (which collectively gross over $40M in revenue annually). Pejman shares a very unique perspective on success and entrepreneurship; one that involves the birth of innovation through the impact made on others as well as the human connections we create daily, backed by years of effective and practical leadership skills. While currently enjoying a very high level of financial freedom, Pejman focuses his efforts on teaching others the importance of self-awareness, belief, and the power of defining their roles and purpose. In his work with the SecretEntourage.com Academy, Pejman has been able to bring together over 200 of today's brightest and most accomplished entrepreneurs in the hopes that their combined efforts will lead to making entrepreneurial education and resources accessible, affordable, and relevant to today's modern and evolving economic climate.

Made in the USA
Columbia, SC
03 July 2017